"Why Me?
Why Not Me?
Thank God, ME!"

— GULSHAN KAVARANA

Kurush Khodaiji

INDIA • SINGAPORE • MALAYSIA

ISBN 979-8-89415-998-0

Acknowledgement

Kurush Khodaiji

My deepest gratitude to Gulshan for having chosen me to write her biography.

The countless video calls, which were a mix of questions, free-flowing conversations, emails, introspection, writing, rewriting, and finally having this finished book in front of you, seem completely worth it!

Why Me? Why Not Me? Thank God, ME!! is exactly how I am feeling right now, knowing that you, dear reader, are about to immerse yourself in the world of Gulshan Kavarana.

It is my privilege to have contributed to this story. One would have never imagined that when we first initiated the process, we would actually have a story that not only highlights the joys and many challenges of the special needs community but also transforms itself into a harbinger of hope and motivation for everyday people – "If you can't find one, start one." is a line that has life-transforming potential.

Gulshan and I would like to extend a big thank you to two very special individuals, Freny and Shenny, for patiently lending us their ears, their expertise, and their time to give us a precious third-person perspective, which was needed after writing the first few drafts.

Thank you, Notion Press and team, for your professionalism and diligence. We could not have found a better publishing partner to launch a book of this nature.

Thank you to all the readers who are destined to read this and for purchasing this book. A double thank you if you've been kind enough to leave us a review. We value it immensely!

Gulshan Kavarana

I am ever so grateful to the divine for making me realise the strength, the kindness, and the compassion that unleashed itself mysteriously.

No words can do justice if I were to thank the numerous people I had the privilege of being around in my darkest period. If it wasn't for all of you, it would have been rather impossible to come out of the "Why Me?" state of anger and pity. My deepest and sincerest appreciation to you special ones for helping me believe and slowly giving me the strength to finally see that indeed "Why Not Me?"

I am what I am today only because of the two pillars of my life, my husband Zeheer and Jenai.

I would not be here today if it were not for the boundless unconditional love of my daughter, Jenai, and the silent but very powerful presence of my husband Zeheer. Their unrelenting and unwavering support is the very reason I could give myself fully to a cause so close to my heart.

Thank you, Kurush, for accepting to write this and give it the vision it needed.

Most importantly, thank you, Zara, for choosing me as your mom!

As you journey through this book, the numerous people I have spoken about will reveal themselves.

Thank you to everyone who has taken the trouble to pick up this book and read our work of love.

This book is dedicated to my daughter

Zara

the one and only reason I happened
to undertake this journey.

- Gulshan Kavarana

Zara is an angel
Zara is a flower
Zara is so beutiful
Zara gives everybody a lot
of power
Zaras always smiling
Zara is the best
and she's never a pest

By
Jas Singh
6 years
3.8.04

Contents

Contents

Chapter - Prelude

In the midst of all the chaos that was taking place, I smiled. I surprised myself—how could I smile when my heart was aching? This was not a smile of joy; it was perhaps one of realisation and acceptance. I sat there, shaken. After long years of pain and suffering, I could still smile.

She had just collapsed again. After a series of seizures, she lay limp in my arms. Her tiny, beautiful face exhausted, her body fatigued. I prayed.

I know every pregnant mother has lingering doubts. What if… what if my child is not normal? I had that doubt too, but then it was a bit like—it can happen to someone else but not me.

Humans, in general, are perennially worried about everything. Sadly, we worry about being 'too' happy. We often equate being 'too' happy with the lull before the storm, like something will go wrong.

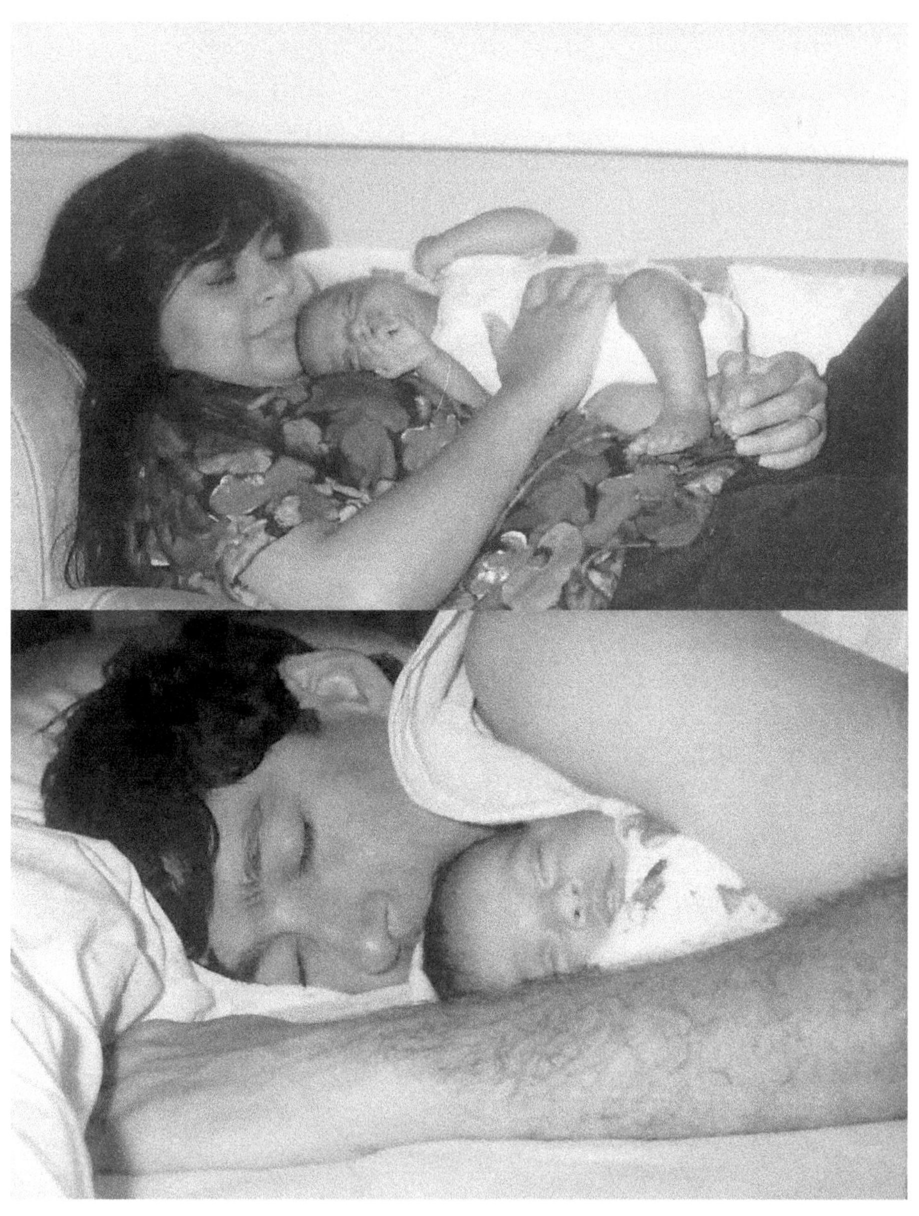

Zara as a new born in 1997 with Zeheer and me

Chapter 1

Thin, Long Fingers

My husband Zeheer and I would finally be together under one roof forever. I could not believe this was happening.

Zeheer is a maritime engineer, and we had spent several years apart after our marriage. The joy of having our first daughter, Jenai, in 1989 was dampened when Zeheer had to sail away soon after. I missed him terribly those years. He finally landed a job at the Dry Docks in Dubai, and we moved there in 1997.

That same year, I was going to become a mother again. The year 1997, in more ways than one, had all the makings of a truly milestone year.

The hospital we chose was called 'Al Zahra'. Strangely enough, our doctor had an uncanny resemblance to my mother! All the boxes were ticking themselves effortlessly.

What would have otherwise been a regular Saturday afternoon suddenly took an unprecedented turn. The pre-scheduled ultrasound test showed placenta previa (the placenta covers the opening in the mother's cervix), and I had to be admitted immediately.

We were simply not prepared for something of this nature. We had barely settled into our new lives, and we found ourselves in an emergency. Arrangements had to be made for Jenai, our older daughter, to be looked after by friends. My husband's office did not grant him leave at such short notice, and suddenly, I found myself all alone in a hospital in an alien land. I was due to deliver at the end of the month, and it was only the 3rd of May. This meant having to spend many lonely days in a hospital away from home.

Just as I was resigning myself to the long wait, there was another unprecedented turn of events. I was told it was imperative to do a C-section as there was danger to both our lives. This really jolted me. It seems I had spoken too soon about the fortunes of the year 1997.

Zara was born on the 5th of May 1997. I distinctly remember waves of panic hitting me as I was wheeled into the operating theatre.

I was barely conscious, but I do remember being wheeled back to my room. Even in this state, the back-of-the-head fear kept playing out.

"Will she be a normal baby?"

I did not even open my eyes and gestured to Zeheer, asking him about our newborn baby. Zeheer instantly understood what I was actually referring to and smiled back with a nod in the affirmative.

"How is she? Say more," I finally had to voice it.

"She has thin, long fingers."

Her hands were covering her face, and that was all that was visible to him. I did not give up. I looked at him, wanting more details.

"She hardly has any hair on her head."

Oh my God! He's not telling me if she is 'normal' or not. That's the only thing I wanted to know then.

She has thin, long fingers.

These words ring in my ears even today. They were the first words I heard from my husband after Zara's delivery.

I was worried sick about Zara's health right after her birth, but I still remember how it amused me greatly that he seemed disappointed about her not having too much hair on her head.

After this ordeal, the arrival of a healthy baby, replaced the panic with bliss.

We named her Zara which means princess.

The way her older sibling Jenai, held her was most heartening. I felt like this was a bond for life.

I left the hospital after six days. By this time my mother had flown in from Mumbai, my in-laws were on their way, and everything seemed perfect all over again. In the days to follow, Zara grew up beautifully.

On second thoughts, maybe I was right about 1997 after all.

Zara's birth annoucement

Chapter 2

Thank You for not Causing
Her Any Pain

July 31, 1997 was a day I will never forget. In fact, a day the world will never forget. We were all forced to sit up and take notice of the unpredictable nature of life.

The beautiful and charming Lady Diana had lost her life in a car accident. For a moment, it seemed like I had just experienced a bad dream. The world was in a state of shock and media across the globe was consumed relaying only this tragedy. Speculation was rife about the circumstances around her death.

I was scheduled to take Zara for her second dose of the DPT vaccination that very afternoon. I wrapped her in a cotton blanket, got into a taxi, and headed to the clinic, still reeling from the news headlines of the day.

The busy paediatrician mechanically waved her hands, pointing me in the general direction of a nurse. The moment she raised her head and looked at me, I demonstrated 'vaccine' in sign language. This action prompted her to point me to the right nurse.

I distinctly remember placing her on a little bed. I winced the moment that monstrous needle was jabbed into her thigh. Yet, to my surprise, there was not a sound from Zara. I waited, just to be sure. She was vaccinated, and she did not cry!

"Thank you," the nurse did not react.

"Thank you for not causing her any pain," she smiled and seemed slightly astonished as to why someone would thank her for a routine jab.

I was so impressed with the nurse's skills that I locked her in a tight hug. She did not fully reciprocate the hug, understandably.

"It's OK! No problem," she smiled back shyly.

We say a lot, we speak, we use words to emote, to fill in empty spaces. Yet often we know that words are just not adequate.

However, strangely, for me this time it was different.

"Thank you for not causing her any pain."

As these words left my lips, I knew I really, truly meant it.

The side-effects in some shape or form were expected from the vaccination but again, I was pleasantly surprised. There was no reaction and no fever. A wave of relief passed through me and after a brief discussion with my husband, we put her to sleep at around ten that night without any medication.

I lay in bed with my eyes closed, coming to terms with the surreal passing away of the world's most adored princess and at the same time, thanking the divine for keeping my little princess safe and healthy.

Chapter 3

Move, Do Something.

Hours passed. I had slipped into dreamless sleep.

I was woken by a sound that I initially thought I was imagining. I was half inclined to go back to sleep, but the sound persisted, and it seemed to be coming from Zara's cot a few feet away. My first instinct was to wake Zeheer, but I let that thought pass, got up, and went to Zara. It was too dark; I could not ascertain what was happening just by the sound.

I quickly found a flashlight and carefully directed it at Zara. It took a good five seconds for my eyes to adjust to the bright light. I saw that her right limbs were shaking. I immediately picked her up and could now actually feel the shaking. I could tell something was just not right. Much as I tried to stay calm, I felt paranoia building up. My experience with volunteering at the Dubai Centre for Special Needs (DCSN) came in handy. I instantly knew this was not normal. I shook my husband awake.

"Hold her. I need to call the doctor."

I was numb with fright.

The doctor, from what she could gather, confirmed to us that it was a convulsion.

I realised how petrified I was when the doctor asked me to check her temperature. My palms had turned icy cold; the phone was shaking in my hand.

I hung up and somehow managed to keep my wits about me. I placed Zara in a bathtub filled with water, not sure if she had a fever.

Zeheer held her in the tub as I called the in-house doctor.

We were living in a plush hotel apartment complex back then, and the doctor at the hotel seemed like the best idea given the situation.

All of a sudden, her jerking stopped and her body went completely limp. We thought we had lost her.

Once again, I found the strength to move past the panic.

"Move, do something," I told myself. "Get dressed quickly. We need to take her to the emergency room."

All the crazy roller-coaster rides paled in comparison with this twenty-minute taxi drive to the hospital. My mind and my emotions were racing faster than the actual speed of the cab. The many bends, steep curves, and the sudden braking of my thoughts made the ride truly arduous.

Zeheer and I sat in silence throughout. Our world was turning upside down, and we had nothing to say to each other. We tried to stay calm despite our internal panic.

Zara had a convulsion, the doctor confirmed it, and she was also running a high fever—104 degrees. He needed to do a lumbar puncture immediately.

To add to our agony, the doctor poked her about five times with no positive result.

She was admitted to the children's ward, and we stayed up the entire night in shock and disbelief. It seemed like a bad dream, and I somehow hoped I would just wake up and put it all behind me.

"There is nothing to worry about. This is a normal reaction to a vaccine. She has suffered a febrile convulsion, which is quite common when children get high fever, especially caused by the triple vaccine." These words gave us immense relief and hope that all would be well.

A febrile convulsion, I learnt, is a fit or seizure that occurs in children aged between 6 months and 6 years when they get a high fever.

I yawned partially out of tiredness and mostly out of relief.

The worst seemed to be behind us. If ever I had wished anything in my life to be prophetic, it would be these words uttered by the doctor. Call it my desire for good news or simply my need to feel normal, I kept repeating these words in my mind over and over again.

I felt my body physically relax, knowing now that the seizure was a one-time occurrence.

Chapter 4

Defiance Meets Denial

Two months later:

It had not even been a few days since we had landed in Mumbai with a five-month-old Zara. October is easily the sultriest month of the year, but we were happy to be there in the midst of family and friends who had known us forever. A much-needed vacation and change of scene for all of us.

It was the auspicious night of Diwali, and we were dining at a friend's place. We easily slipped back into 'hometown' mode: laughter, leg-pulling, and many inside jokes best enjoyed in our local lingo. It had been a tough few months in Dubai, and I was slowly getting into my element. I was home, and I was going to make the most of it. Amidst peals of laughter, I remembered I had to nurse Zara, though all I really wanted was to be out there in the thick of the action. Anyway, it was only a matter of time before I could join the party again.

As I was nursing Zara, smiling to myself, I felt her head moving strangely. At first, I did not make much of it, but after quick repeated occurrences, I realised she was having a mouth spasm, a seizure while I was nursing her. Convulsions normally come with fever, but she had no fever.

Our fun evening took an unexpected turn, and we found ourselves outside the paediatric Intensive Care Unit of our neighbourhood hospital. Zara was having one seizure after another. This was her second episode after the first one in Dubai post-being vaccinated.

Zeheer and I sat up all night in the car and found ourselves in shock and panic all over again. We finally got to see our baby at the crack of dawn. It broke my heart to see her like this. Though pale and wan, she was in a mood to play. The seizures had ceased. We ran through the routine tests, the CT scan, etc., and due to a lack of any concrete findings, we were told it was probably a metabolic disorder.

After the initial bout of feeling helpless and going through the anxiety once again, I decided to call my cousin's wife, a doctor at a reputed hospital in Mumbai. I wanted to shift Zara there, but there were absolutely no beds available.

"Put her under a bed, any bed. I don't care."

I was desperate to shift Zara into a better facility. I was willing to go to any lengths.

I asked for a premature discharge from the hospital and was met with much resistance. This was one scary gamble, as there was no guarantee of us finding a room elsewhere. The doctor and the administrative staff were up in arms. They were aghast and offended. How could I do such a thing?

They finally agreed, but it was with much reluctance under what is known as DAMA – Discharged Against Medical Advice. As the discharge procedure was taking place, I was categorically told that "We will not touch your child even if she were to have a seizure." My decision, it seemed, had hurt a few egos. Their prophetic words rang true, and as we were leaving, Zara began having another seizure. They remained true to their word and did not attend to her.

We rushed her to the emergency room at the hospital where my cousin's wife is a practising consultant and finally managed a shared room with another patient. This was when the reputed neurologist, Dr. Vrajesh Udani, entered our lives.

As soon as Dr. Udani saw her, he scribbled SMEI on his notepad. I also saw him put two question marks after that.

"What does this mean?"

"Severe myoclonic epilepsy in infancy."

He also went on to mention that multiple other tests would need to be carried out to rule out any other possibilities.

He prescribed medication which Zara would be on, and we would consult him on an ongoing basis.

"The prognosis does not look very good. She is going to regress."

It was almost as if I had conveniently forgotten the meaning of the word 'regress'. I simply did not believe him.

"Will she get better?" I shot back.

That was not really a question as much as a lie, a false reassurance I needed to hear.

"Worse." This was like an arrow piercing through my heart.

He asked me if I had any questions.

Little did he expect that I would come up with two hundred questions, written on full-scape sheets of paper, leaving enough space for him to write the answers. I have to admire his patience and care for answering all of them.

SMEI came to be more popularly known as Dravet's syndrome after a French doctor named Charlotte Dravet did extensive research on it. Dravet syndrome is a very complex form of epilepsy, and unfortunately, no cure has yet been found. But it is only thanks to her and her exhaustive work that it can now be diagnosed as separate and distinct from other types of epilepsy.

Diwali is associated with joy and light but ours descended into the pit of darkness.

I am not the type to give up. I was determined to fight. How could God do this to her? How could fate treat us this cruelly?

I was going to prove them all wrong. My daughter would emerge victorious. I would not let her down.

This was the beginning of my defiance and denial. I had to find a way to believe, else I would crumble.

"I challenge you, world," I said silently to myself.

It happened again. We found ourselves rushing Zara to the emergency room, where she would remain in the Intensive Care Unit for a full seven days. She had another seizure, and although she had no fever, I could sense that this time it was more serious than the previous one.

Our hope of finding a diagnosis by way of an MRI, EEG, and CT scans all proved to be futile; nothing showed up.

Zara's toothless smile disappeared. My happy, bubbly child was slowly turning into a 'zombie', just staring into space.

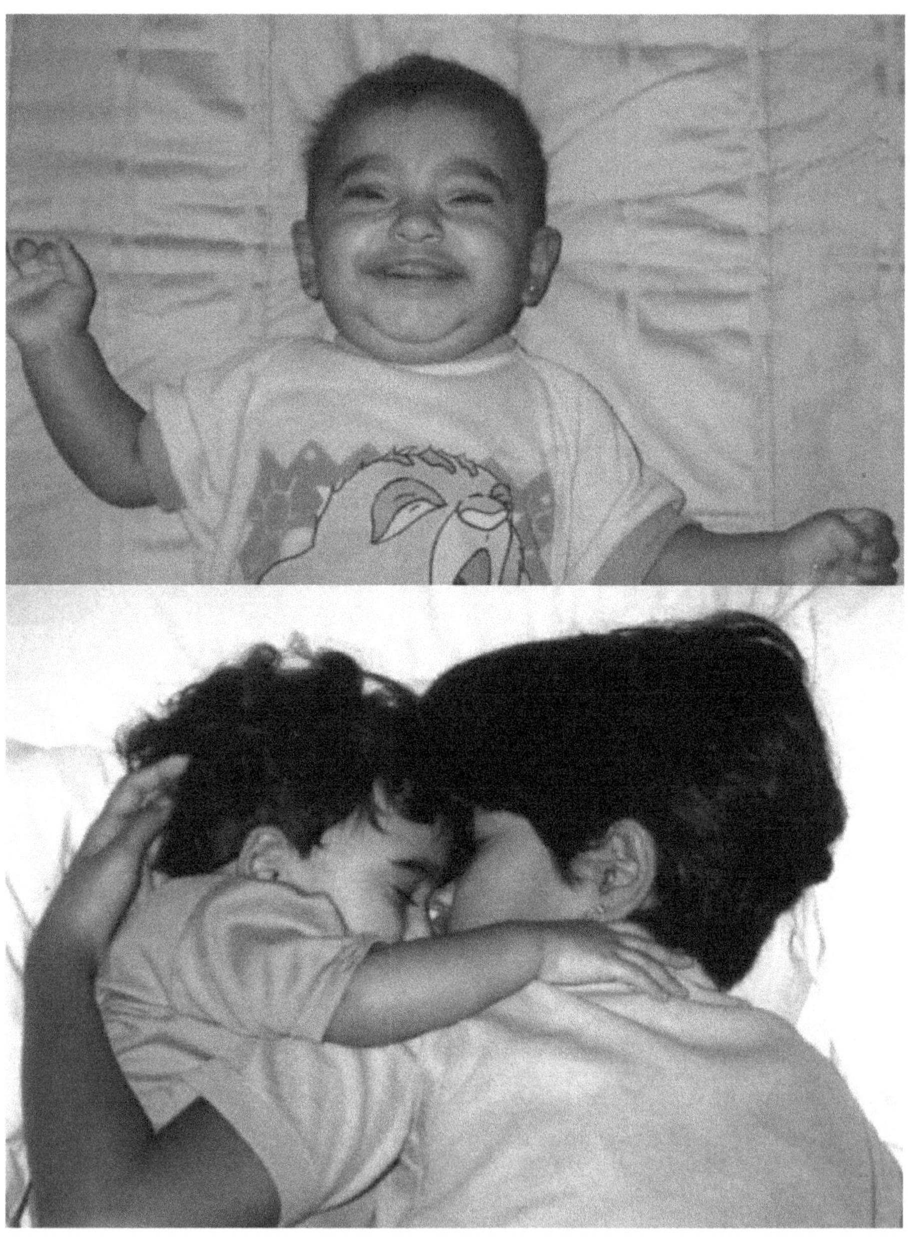

Zara finding love, warmth and support in Jenai's arms

Chapter 5

Regression

Twenty-seven years have passed, and to this day, her seizures are relentless in their regularity. They are an integral part of our lives, part of our very being. We've tried all kinds of medication; nothing seems to work.

Somewhere along the way, I subconsciously developed a "selective hearing" syndrome. It was the only way I could remain sane by somehow weeding out what I did not want to hear.

The doctor in Mumbai had used the word "regression" for Zara's situation. I am not sure if I was naïve or if I chose to act like I was, but I did not quite comprehend what was being communicated. I simply let that comment slip out of my ears like I had never heard it.

I started feeling conflicting emotions towards my doctor. Dr. Udani once mentioned to my cousin's wife, his colleague at the hospital, "I think Gulshan sees me as a devil."

I would often say to myself, "Why does this man say things about Zara which would never come true?"

From toxic hatefulness, when I felt no hope, to absolute adoration when I saw the remotest glimmer of hope. Rationality at a time like this was beyond my psychological and emotional capacity. I was willing to do anything as long as they could cure my Zara.

As much as I wanted to escape the reality of the situation, it was evident that Zara was on the decline.

She had a limited vocabulary of six meaningful words, namely "hot" when pointing to a cup with a hot beverage. She would point with her finger and say "this" and would also occasionally say "that." She would point to the foot and say "shoes," body parts like eyes and ears, and then last but not least, she affectionately called her father "dada." I fondly remember how she would sing it out like "dadaaaa." Zara's development and progress were nowhere close to the other children her age.

My spirit was breaking with every passing day. I have heard people talk about pain and slow death. You think you understand the depths of another's suffering when it is narrated to you, but truth be told, until something as shattering as this happens to you, you have no idea of the dimension or, for that matter, the magnitude of someone else's suffering. I finally actually felt it, felt suffering in its breadth and its depth. This began and ended with me; me, isolated and alone.

"The seizures were overtaking our lives, As an artist I began to draw what was overwhelming me. I had to get it out of my system"

- Gulshan Kavarana

Chapter 6

A Gentle Presence

One afternoon, I sat exhausted, sad, and for the most part relieved that we had an afternoon to ourselves, a lull. Zara seemed peaceful. Stillness enveloped the room. My attention fell upon a gentle presence.

This person took Zara into his arms and held her like there was nothing else in the world but her. To him, she was a perfect creation. I could not take my eyes off him. My gaze fixated like a smitten teenager who had fallen in love all over again. That afternoon embodied my life. I was in that moment and nowhere else. I felt what I had never felt before: conflicting emotions of acceptance, along with a hint of fear and an underlying uncertainty of what was to follow. And yet, this strange combination seemed to complete me.

Zeheer looked at me and smiled as if he had read my thoughts. I did not feel the need to verbally communicate anything to him. Every storm, every lull, and everything in between flashed right in front of me. I learnt another important lesson that day: amazing things happen in the lap of silence.

I thanked the universe a hundred times over for his gentle and giving presence. When I looked at him, I knew he felt a love for Zara that was simply there—unquestioned and accepting.

I choked up as I looked at him, the father of my daughters. I would never again let the chaos of our situation take over the beauty of what destiny had intended for us.

I watched as he held Zara and, for a fleeting moment, I could not help but wonder: was he holding her, or was she holding him?

And thus began the journey, the road to someplace.

Zara was eleven months old, just a month shy of turning one. By this point, we had been living with the uncertainty of seizures for almost a year.

Was there not some way out? I prided myself on fixing situations, on finding solutions. Something had to happen—a path had to emerge. This was a long, dark tunnel, and somehow, I had to find the light.

My mind went back to a term I had been introduced to by Dr. Udani. He had warned me about 'Doctor Shopping.'

"Gulshan, do not fall into this vicious trap. It will suck you in completely."

I chose to hear only what I wanted to. I heard him but refused to believe him. There had to be a doctor in some corner of the world who could save my daughter by miraculously curing her.

A vicious trap? In hindsight, yes.

I went 'doctor shopping' like a person possessed. The journey had begun.

Doctors from across the globe got involved. Zara's reports were sent far and wide to six different states within the USA, to Canada, to France, to the United Kingdom, and to doctors all over India. All this was done in the hope that somehow, someone, somewhere would prove Dr. Udani's diagnosis wrong and actually have a solution.

Hundreds of opinions, sadly the same diagnosis: that of Dr. Udani.

By this time, Zeheer and I had stopped pretending and were totally shattered. This should have been the time to keep going and not give up, or completely accept the situation as was told to us by renowned doctors worldwide. It was none of that. Instead, I moved to self-pity and victimhood.

"Why me? Why has life chosen this for me? I am alone."

I was hurting and drowning in self-pity. In order to justify feeling like the victim, I started to feel isolated.

This stage lasted a few months. I exchanged several conversations with God. Cure her, and I will do…this and that and that. I gave up wearing any kind of jewellery, saying I would only wear it once Zara was well.

This stage of self-pity lasted a while. I remember the day it changed.

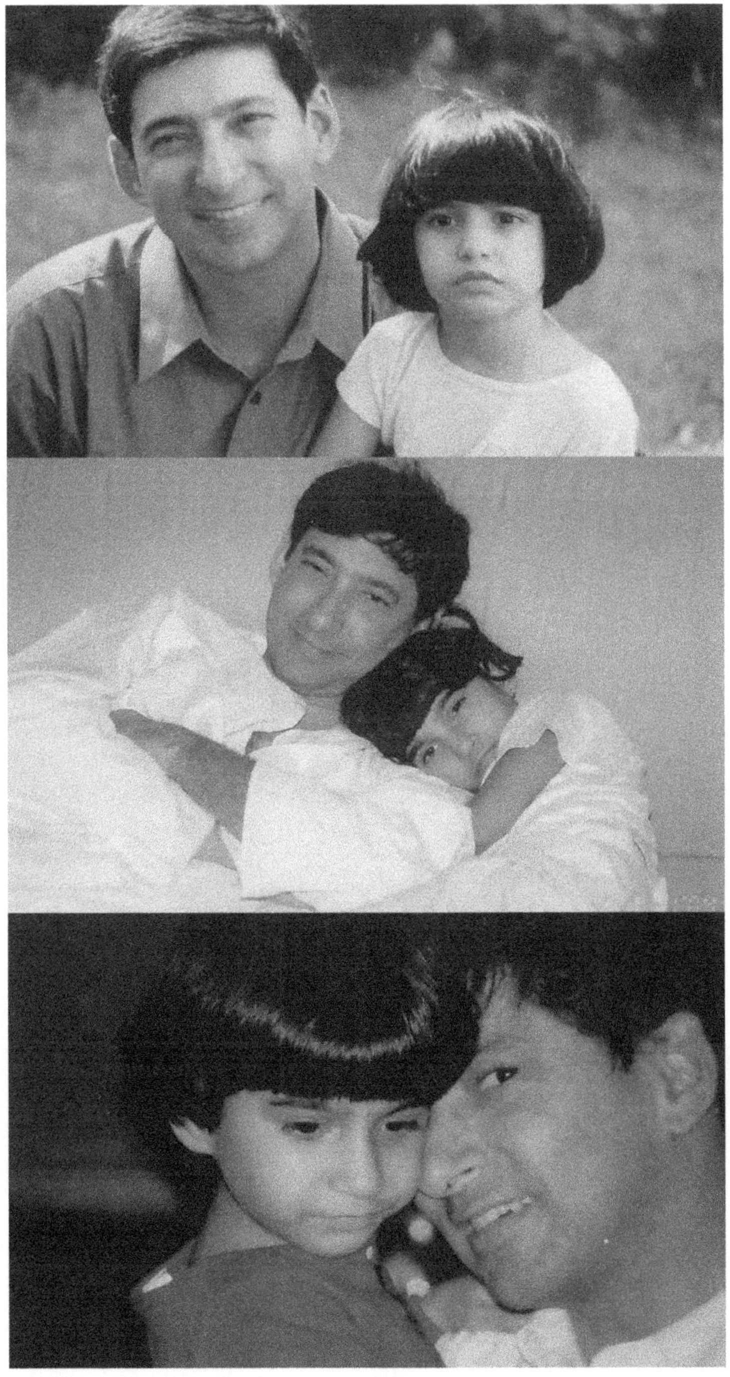

Daddy's Girl

Chapter 7

I Have Twin Daughters

The doorbell rang. Strangers were at my door.

"Hello, I am Sandhya," she said. There was a radiance in her smile, and she had a remarkable aura.

Along with a middle-aged man, she walked into my posh, fully carpeted hotel apartment. Minutes later, we were all sitting on my plush sofa.

I always believed I was a person who would never be affected by the material things of life; but I realised after our move to Dubai that it mattered. I felt special and very privileged in our upward move. This was a lifestyle different from what I was used to in Mumbai. It gave me a sense of false superiority. Maybe it also acted as a shield against the pain I was experiencing with Zara.

Sandhya Perera was a qualified teacher trained in Montessori for children with special needs. She was an early interventionist, and given Zara's condition, I should have welcomed her. Sadly, my attitude was dismissive and full of disdain.

"I know what you are going through," she said, her tone soft and her demeanour calm.

"No, you don't. Do you even know what epilepsy is?" I shot back.

She flashed that beautiful smile again, but in my state of rage and frustration, I completely missed its beauty.

She paused, smiled again, looked me right in the eye and said, "I have twin daughters. They both have cerebral palsy, and one of them gets seizures quite regularly."

I could not believe what I had just heard. I found myself off my swanky sofa, on the ground with my hands on her knees, apologising profusely for my despicable behaviour.

Sandhya's truth had humbled me and brought me down to reality. I felt in awe of this good, simple woman.

Very soon we were deep in conversation. I felt thankful for her presence. I knew this was the beginning of something wonderful. Finally, someone genuinely understood what I was going through, better perhaps than I understood it myself.

We went on to work tirelessly, with fierce determination. We did extensive research on relevant interventions and chose a good speech therapist for Zara.

Sandhya Perera turned out to be my saviour. She was exactly what I needed at that point.

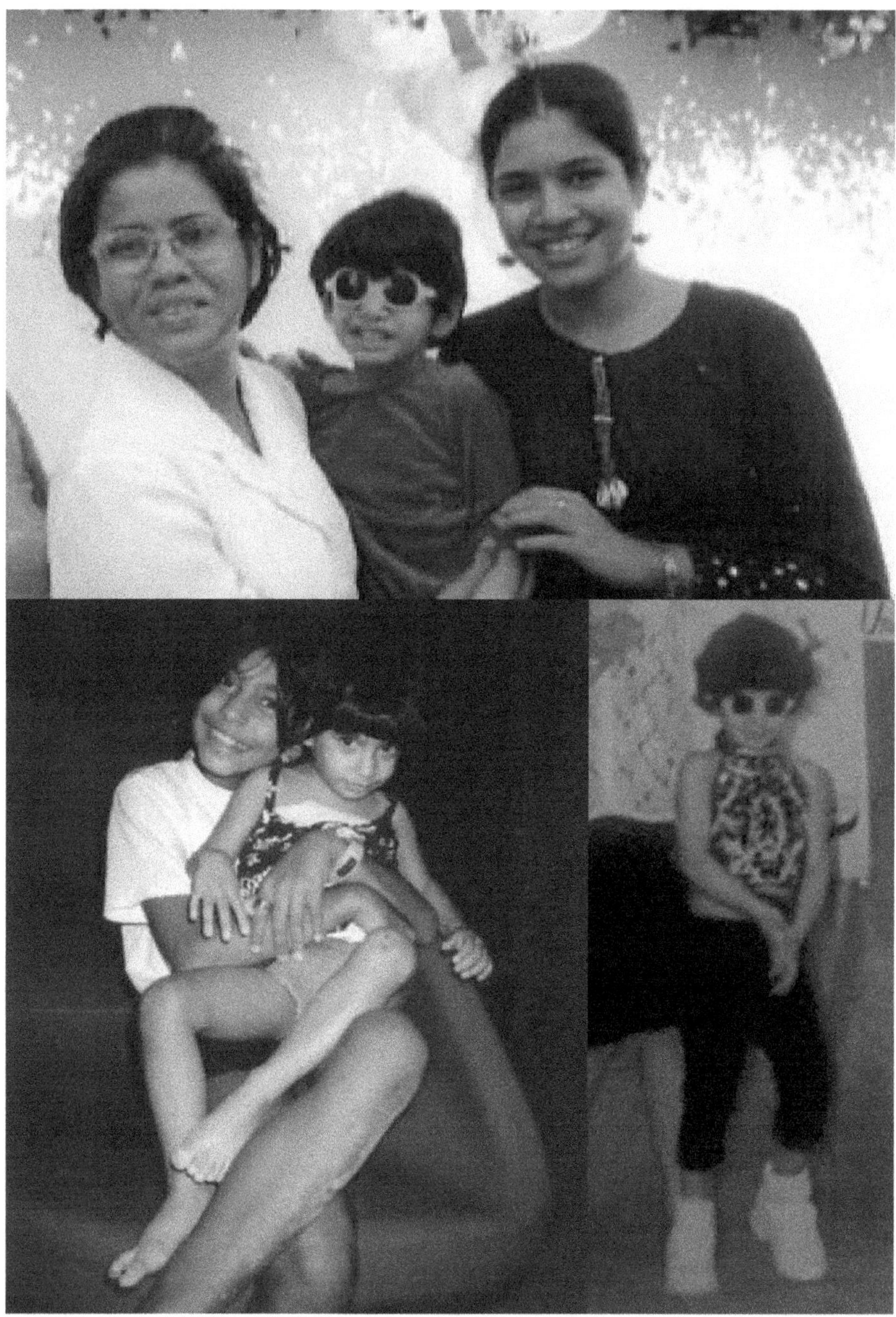

Top: *Zara with her favourite teachers, Sandhya and Vanessa* | Bottom Left: *Zara and Jenai in the park after sunset so that she could be without her glasses* | Bottom Right: *Zara on stage at a SFS event with her dark glasses*

Chapter 8

Don't Turn on the Lights.

I am no insomniac, have never been one, but I was sleep deprived. This was not about a couple of nights here and there, but an entire fourteen months.

Zara could not sleep. She would just be up all night, every night. When she slept, it would be piecemeal, an hour perhaps in the morning and then again for a little while at other times of the day. There was simply no predictable pattern to this. There were days when she was having about nine seizures on average.

On multiple occasions, we found Zara attracted like a honeybee to any source of light. She would look straight into the source of light, be it a light bulb or sunlight streaming into the room, and instantly her head would begin jerking. She began getting seizures every time she looked at bright lights.

It was soon confirmed that she was photosensitive. At first, we began to dim the lights, thinking it would be easier that way, but quickly realised that any light, even dim light, caused her seizures to suddenly appear out of nowhere.

Our hotel apartment had the most spectacular sunset view, and heartbreakingly, I was always pulling down the blinds. These blinds would virtually be down for the next three years. We practically spent our life in darkness.

This was a new low for me: the darkness within and the darkness outside.

I really began looking forward to the odd outing with my husband, Zeheer, my older daughter, Jenai, and Zara; it was also a way to spend time and bond with my older daughter. We needed to feel "normal" again, even if it was for just a little bit.

All the excitement would vanish as invariably we ended up cancelling at the last minute due to a sudden seizure or finding Zara in no position to handle an outing of any sort. Our friends understood this but ended up making me feel even guiltier about not spending enough time with my older daughter. She never complained, but we were missing out on activities that we used to do as a family.

When they mentioned how much "fun" they had, it would hurt me deeply. On one hand, I held nothing against them after all we were a bunch of young couples wanting to explore a new life in a new country. On the other hand, it also frustrated me and heightened our situation even more. Why was I not having fun?

Attending birthday parties of "normal" children was unbearable. I smiled through it all, but deep inside I was angry and hurt. The lack of sleep over a long period of time was magnifying every emotion.

I thought acting like everything was fine would somehow make it go away. Initially, every time Zara had a seizure, I would call up my husband at work and let him know. Later, I just stopped. He would come back from the office and ask about her, and I would just say she is fine, when nothing was fine, not her, and certainly not me. It was all building up.

I was in a constant state of flux. At one level, I would rationalise that it was not correct to feel this resentment and anger towards the world. A few moments later, I would flip and somehow justify it. There was nowhere to go and no place to hide.

I had to find some form of escape. The supermarket on the ground floor of our hotel became just that for me. If ever I could find even twenty spare minutes, I would run down in a heartbeat.

This escape, however, came with an annoying initial hurdle. The well-meaning employees at the store, out of genuine concern, would unfailingly inquire about Zara and her health. I cannot fault them for doing so, but damn it, this was meant to be my escape where I forgot about my reality for just a little bit, and here they were reminding me of it. I had to eventually tell them not to ask about Zara. Many understood, but some felt rather offended.

I am a creative person with a degree in commercial art, and not being able to conceptualise, design, or just paint added to my overall bleakness. I craved a creative outlet. I would aimlessly walk around the store and just pick up products off the shelves or simply admire their labels. I would imagine how I would have designed them differently. I would do this repeatedly with an array of products and completely lose myself in this process. This was my escape. This was my therapy.

In time, the employees and I struck a friendship of sorts. They realised I loved looking at architecture and design magazines. They let me borrow magazines and joked with me that never before had the store been used as a library.

The escape ended as soon as I was back in the apartment.

I wrote a hundred letters to God, telling Him how much I hated Him for putting me through this.

"Accept you are in a difficult situation," Sandhya's words rang in my ears. Now I knew just how difficult.

I was breaking down. Nothing was working.

4   *Emirates*   GULF NEWS

For little Zara, it's a semi-dark world

Three-year-old suffers from acute photosensitivity due to brain damage blamed on DPT injection

By Joanna Langley

Dubai

Despite living in one of the sunniest places on earth, little Zara Kavarana exists in a semi-dark world where she may never be able to watch television, or enjoy a day at the beach.

The three-year-old girl suffers from acute photosensitivity caused by brain damage, and has seizures if she is exposed to light – a condition her mother claims is the result of a routine vaccination administered when she was four months old.

Gulshan Kavarana, 36, said her child was "a normal healthy baby" before her second injection of DPT in 1997, which is for whooping cough, diphtheria and tetanus.

The DPT vaccine is given to children in a series of three injections at the ages of two, four, and six months, and has been known to cause serious side effects including brain damage.

Kavarana, who lives in Dubai, said that within a matter of hours of her second jab, Zara was rushed to hospital suffering from a seizure and a high fever.

"Until Zara had the injection, she was like any other baby, but within 16 hours of the vaccine she began to shake uncontrollably and her temperature soared.

"After a few hours she seemed okay, and we hoped the fit was a one off incident. Within a matter of weeks, she had another fit.

"She's now had more than 400, some of which can last for an hour. The seizures happen because her brain is hypersensitive to light and the smallest amount will set her off. Her speech is delayed and we suspect she may now be mentally retarded."

Kavarana said she does not blame the hospital where the injection was given, and has not lodged a formal complaint. But although most of the doctors who have seen Zara say her condition started coincidentally after her second injection, Kavarana is convinced otherwise.

Risky element

"So far, nobody has been able to give me any other explanation for Zara's condition. Her disability is the result of brain damage and the vaccine is the most probable cause."

Dr. Rita Kovesdi, a paediatrician at the Dubai London Clinic, said that although serious adverse reactions to the DPT injection were rare, they did happen, and could result in brain damage.

"There is a one in 100,000 chance of the injection causing an extreme reaction in a child, which usually happens within a 72-hour time frame.

"The whooping cough component is the most risky element of the vaccine. It can cause encephalopathy, a very high temperature and seizures. The adverse reaction usually happens after the second injection because the body becomes extremely sensitive from the first jab."

Kovesdi said although a new safer version of the vaccine, called DPAT, is now available in some private clinics in Dubai, many children are still vaccinated using DPT.

The new DPAT vaccine, which has only been available for a few months, dramatically reduces the risk of adverse side effects, but some parents still continue to use the old one, she pointed out.

"Some choose it because of the cost element – the new one is approximately double the price of DPT – and others sometimes opt for it because their child did not suffer any reaction with the first injection.

"However, the damage is often caused by the second injection, so this doesn't mean a child will not react."

Kovesdi said clinics administering any vaccine should inform parents of the possible side effects. "Parents should be asked if their child has suffered from any allergic reactions to antibiotics, eggs or any past vaccine, and they should also be told of the risks."

She added that although DPT has been known to cause serious side effects, it was extremely rare, and it was still far safer to vaccinate children.

"Babies do die from whooping cough, tetanus and diphtheria, and vaccination is very necessary. I vaccinated my own child with DPT because at that time DPAT was not available. But one child in 100,000 being affected adversely is one child too many. I would advise parents who are worried to use DPAT, which is much safer."

Changed life

Kavarana said her daughter's life had been 'ruined by the vaccine' and that she wished the new version had been available to her.

"Our lives have changed completely as a result of Zara's condition. My 10-year-old daughter has to do her homework in darkness because any amount of light will make Zara have a fit.

"We cannot have a television, enjoy a family outing, or even visit friends' houses. I feel terribly guilty because I allowed her to have the injections in the first place.

"If DPAT had been available three years ago, I definitely would have opted for it. Parents should be aware that the new vaccine is better, and should make sure they know about the side effects of vaccines."

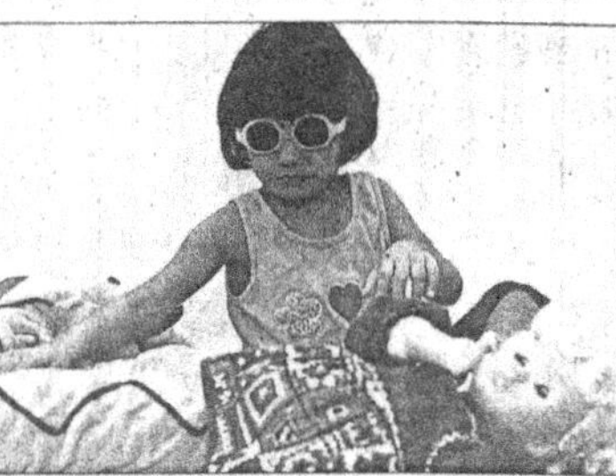

Three-year old Zara wears dark shades as she plays in her room. – GN picture by Victoria Calaguian

Article in the Gulf News
June 24, 2000

Chapter 9

"There Must Be Something in Your Milk."

Dr. Udani made the big mistake of asking me if I had any questions for him. I said I had a few. He asked me to write them down and he would answer them.

I did as he said. I began writing on full scape paper, the kind students use for their school and college examinations in India. I would write a question and leave a gap on the sheet for his answer, and then proceed to write my next question. I wrote for what could be best described as an eternity. I had not one, not two, but two hundred questions for the doctor. I presented what resembled a booklet comprising two hundred questions manually checked and rechecked by me for spelling and grammar. This booklet was dearer than life itself.

A challenging phase of my life was round the corner, one I had not anticipated—dealing with not just people, but people close to me: family and friends.

"There must be something in your milk."

Did I hear that correctly?

"There must be something in your milk. Each time you nurse her, she gets a seizure."

"You must have been unhappy during your pregnancy. These things affect the child," said another.

I was taken aback hearing those harsh words. I had become the centrepiece in people's lives. Zara's condition had become a matter of speculation and conjecture. In all fairness, the family, the extended family, and all our close friends were truly concerned, yet could not see it for what it was. Everyone expected a "normal" baby, and Zara was not "normal."

The subtle, and not so subtle, criticism bordering on blame for what I ought to have done began taking a huge toll on me. These callous and unthinking remarks went round in my brain for days on end. I was a dam ready to burst. It was exhausting enough dealing with the unpredictability of Zara's seizures; the family's misplaced negativity was driving me to the edge.

Dr. Lalkaka, also a neurologist and known to the family, who was treating Zara, came over for lunch on my invitation. I had also invited our extended family. I had an agenda—Dr. Lalkaka dispelled every notion with ease; it was not my milk, nor was it my supposed unhappiness during pregnancy, or other misconceptions my family had. He made them see it for what it was: Zara's condition had nothing to do with me.

Dr. Lalkaka left, and everyone around the table was silent. Finally, the dam broke and the floodgates opened. I began crying like a child. The pent-up pressure of being judged and just dealing with the entire ordeal finally caught up with me. My family rallied around me, with my mother-in-law holding me close. My family started accepting Zara's condition.

The crying did provide relief, but it was temporary.

Top: *My support system - my mother, Perin and mother-in-law Aran*
Bottom: *Zara with my father-in-law Noshir. Zara was his favourite person*

Chapter 10

"So What, She is Still My Sister."

Jenai, my older daughter's selfless contribution in those times was beyond anything I can put into words. Zeheer, my husband, loved Zara unconditionally but was in complete denial of her condition, just like me. However, my older daughter, all of seven, had totally accepted her sister just the way she was from day one.

"So, what, she is still my sister."

Jenai's sensitivity, her understanding of the dynamic of our life, was so on point that it still amazes me as to how deeply she understood what was needed.

I would be looking for clothes in my cupboard, and to my surprise, I would suddenly find a bright pink heart-shaped post-it with the words "she will be fine" written on it.

I would find positive messages in my personal drawer, on the kitchen table, and on my bathroom mirror.

I would find all of Jenai's handiwork after she had left in the morning for school. This was her way of telling me she was always there with me.

Zara would not sleep a wink at night, and even when she did sleep after 6 am, it would be in bouts of twenty minutes here and there. It had been fourteen months of sleep deprivation on the trot. As a result, I could not give Jenai the attention she deserved as a child.

Jenai's most invaluable contribution to us back then was her deep understanding of the situation. When I look back on the trying times, I marvel at her maturity, way beyond her age. As a child, she could have chosen to feel deprived, angry or upset and could very easily have viewed all of this very differently. Instead, by her behaviour, her unconditional love and her sense of responsibility, she actually alleviated our guilt of neglecting her as parents. She understood Zara needed us much more.

Jenai had an unshakeable bond of sisterhood with Zara, but she also took on semi-parental responsibility on many an occasion. She would call her "Zaru Baby." She would often sleep next to her the entire night, never shying away even at the frightening sight of the seizures. She would tear up but never leave her side.

Even today, Jenai will drop anything to be there for her sister. There was a time when getting an online appointment with a prominent doctor was near impossible. We were at a complete loss, and Jenai would just go and sit outside his clinic, wait for hours on occasion, and get us on a video call with the doctor.

She went out of her way to find out about and attend Special Needs Support group meetings to gather as much information as she could. I remember in New York, she met with a professor who was working on a trial drug.

Exposing herself to what other support groups, research centres, and individuals focusing on special needs research were doing, especially in different parts of the globe, helped us to stay abreast of the latest happenings.

We found Jenai taking great interest in learning how to play the guitar. I was taken aback with her dedication to pick it up so quickly all by herself. It is only later that we decided she should learn from a professional musician to make her more proficient.

As a teenager, Jenai kept insisting that we buy her a guitar.

We kept up the denial, typically as parents of growing children often do.

Jenai simply wouldn't give up.

"When we go to Mumbai for your saree wearing ceremony, with all the money you get as gifts, you can buy it with that" she agreed and the matter came to a close.

Jenai put her money where her mouth was- all of fourteen years old, and sure enough, she managed to buy herself a guitar.

Often, I would find some pretty amazing sounding tunes coming out of Jenai's room and thought them to be well reproduced covers of songs an ignorant mother would not be privy to, but these were originally composed songs for Zara on the guitar.

Jenai has written and composed several songs, all devoted to Zara and her condition. She would often sing them to her while playing the guitar. 'Be Careful' is the first song she created for Zara on her own. It will always have a special place in all our hearts.

Jenai had chosen Art as her main subject for her 'A' Level studies. Whenever possible, Jenai would make Zara her subject for all her art school projects.

A project worth mentioning was one on travel, and most of the class had submitted artwork on the different kinds of suitcases, travel bags and the like.

Jenai had created a whole project and called it 'Travel- An Artistic Journey for Zara'. The journey was described through the Latin word 'Fundus' which means Bottom. She attempted to deep dive into what Zara would have to say about her own journey if she could speak for herself. Her work on this project made her Zara's voice.

Jenai has been as involved as Zeheer and me in Zara's upbringing.

"Jenai, get dressed. We have to go out."

Zara would get a seizure, and our lives would change in a matter of minutes. The getting ready to go out, not just with us but with her own friends and then cancelling, became a regular part of all our lives and not once did she ever say, "Not again, mom."

"Go with your friends," I'd urge her to go.

"Are you going? No, right? I'll stay, too."

Jenai loves Zara unconditionally to this day.

Our home could easily have entered the Guinness Book of World Records for having holy water from almost every corner of the planet stacked in bottles on a table. We were advised by well-wishers to dab some on Zara's head, and in our blind quest to see her well somehow, we would comply at the cost of making her squirm. I had to do this. The doctors had to be wrong. Also, the fear of being judged for not trying everything and not caring enough played a huge part.

I self-imposed the role of superwoman on myself and denied help from any quarter. Zeheer was concentrating on his new job in Dubai which was entirely different to his previous experience in the merchant navy. I did not want him to feel burdened in the slightest for that could mean us thinking of moving back to Mumbai where we have our support base. I was convinced Dubai was the better option for us as a family and it was also more suitable in terms of facilities for individuals with special needs.

Jenai and Zara sharing a special bond

Dearest Zara,

Our relationship is like no other... it's a really extraordinary one, one that has no fights, no hatred... only love. Thank you so much for being a vital part of my life; I don't know where I would be without you.

I want you to know that I am and always will be there for you. No matter what... just say 'hmmmm' and I'll be there.

You are an amazing sister and for that I hope that you have positive energies and good vibrations with you today on your very special day and always... HAPPY ROJ BIRTHDAY! You are surrounded by people who love you. Cherish it.

Love you forever
Jenai

Jenai's birthday message to Zara

Travel. for this unit I decided to explore the journey of my sister's life in an artistic form. My sister Zara got brain damaged after her DPT vaccination when she was a mere four months old.

The path that she lives on is very different from ours. It's more pure, more serene... I wanted to portray her travels in my 'art diary'.

In this journal I plan to explore all aspects of my sister's conditional. I would look at brain scans, CT scans, X rays, genes, cells... linking back to my unit 1, natural forms section where I looked at cells.

Jenai's art projects always had Zara as her subject

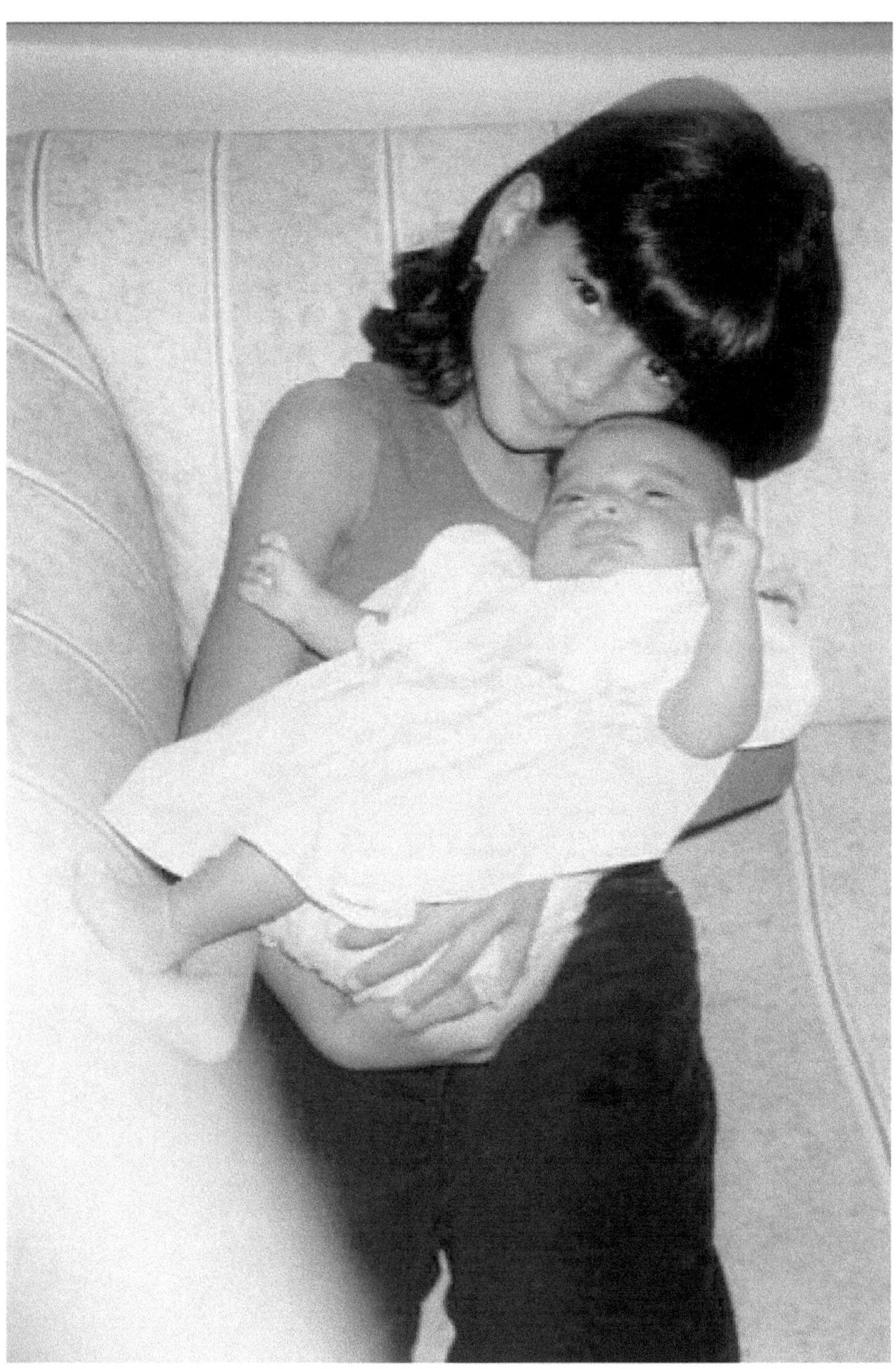

Jenai and Zara when she just got home from the hospital

Chapter 11

Acceptance

My formative years had been spent in the northern Indian city of Lucknow with my paternal uncle and his family. I grew up with my cousins and we moved to Mumbai in the year 1972. My mother, my older sister, and I moved into a Parsi colony (Parsi is the name given to the community of Zoroastrians residing in India) in Mumbai.

I spent my formative years growing up in Mumbai, India's financial capital. The promise of prosperity meant that individuals and families from all corners of the country made it their home. However, most of my friends and my social and religious influences were strongly from within the Parsi colony. It was only when we moved to Dubai that I experienced a true cosmopolitan lifestyle. I began spending time socially with people from all over India and other parts of the world.

Owing to Zara's condition, the conversation often revolved around how to stay positive, whether to follow superstitious beliefs and so on. I was overwhelmed. What should we do? What can we do?

I had a long way to go, but a certain level of acceptance of Zara's condition had entered my mind and heart. Though there was acceptance, deep down inside, I was still fighting. I was of the view that surrendering meant defeat, and hence, something within me was simply refusing to surrender.

My "seeking" was nothing more than a desperate journey, running helter-skelter, hoping salvation would come our way, somehow.

It took me years and many breakdowns to realise the true meaning of the old cliché "accept." I was a work in progress. Acceptance, like a river, takes its own curves and bends, difficult but flowing towards something.

Chapter 12

The Grid

Zeheer, Jenai and I found ourselves in a large dimly lit living room. The place had an eerie energy about it but we had nothing to lose.

A Caucasian woman in her sixties walked towards us and asked us to follow her into her special chamber. As we got up from our seats, she asked my daughter to remain seated as only Zeheer and I would be allowed into the chamber. I could see the disappointment on Jenai's face. Zara had to be our primary focus, and we were willing to go to any lengths to cure her.

We left Jenai and headed into an even more dimly lit chamber. Neither of us felt very comfortable, but we decided to see what the lady had to offer.

After the 'Zara conversation', the same story I had by now repeated on a loop, ad nauseam over a zillion times, a 'studied' silence filled the room. Zeheer and I waited on her solution. The lady presented us with a customised grid drawn on a piece of paper, which we were instructed to place below Zara's pillow, and "everything would be back to normal."

Was this the miracle? Nothing changed. Nothing was meant to change. As expected, we were dejected with the outcome.

Over time, well-wishers had asked us to try everything from mantras to prayers to an array of religious offerings. We did everything.

Zara and I painting

Chapter 13

TOKEN 27000

My father-in-law, who absolutely adored his grand-daughter and was dying to somehow see her miraculously transformed insisted we travel to Rishikesh, one of India's holiest cities and meet this particular Ayurvedic doctor who specialised in curing epilepsy.

We landed in Rishikesh and were completely taken in by the vibe. The Beatles had their contribution in making this city hugely popular all over the world. In the February of 1968, the popular band members travelled to India and in their quest for answers found themselves in Rishikesh.

The waiting area of the clinic was a large space with a grand looking fish tank in the middle of it. We registered ourselves and were given our token number 27000.

Zeheer and I looked at each other in shock. Were there actually 27000 people ahead of us? This was going to take a month at the least. Thankfully, minutes later, we were asked to meet with the doctor. I was expecting an old, bearded man dressed in religious attire, but I was surprised when a pleasant-looking, contemporarily dressed man wearing a bright yellow tweety bird tie welcomed us. I was relieved. This seemed perfect – what better than a modern-day Ayurvedic doctor?

The tiredness of the long journey from Dubai to Rishikesh began to disappear, and my hopes began to rise once again.

The number 27000 on the token was not our waiting number, but in fact, the number of people he had cured of epilepsy to date. We were over the moon.

"I will show the world." I smiled as I said this to myself. I thought of all the naysayers, especially all those supposedly brilliant minds who could not do a thing for my daughter. To hell with accepting defeat. This is onward and upward.

Everything takes time. We had patiently waited for years. I could feel it in my bones –this was our moment.

The doctor handed us the medication, and it was a done deal; in a few days, Zara would stop getting those nasty seizures.

We left the clinic relieved and overjoyed. We attended the famous aarti ceremony where you offer flowers an d a lit diya into the mighty Ganges. We imagined epilepsy leaving Zara's system forever as we blissfully watched the diya with our offerings of flowers float away from us gently wobbling into the holy river, merging with the divine.

Days later, after our return from the ultimate holy trip, a friend casually inquired about our trip. I gave her the details of the meeting and our amazing stay.

We were on a high. We reached our home in Mumbai and were warmly greeted by family and friends.

"We have found a cure for Zara. She's going to be all right."

The loudest and boldest proclamation we ever made for Zara. Our happiness knew no bounds.

We flew back to Dubai, and we said the same thing to our group of well-wishers there.

Word spread that the family had visited Rishikesh, and the atmosphere was such that everyone in the know was anticipating a miracle. It was just a matter of a few days before the magic of the medicine would kick in and change everything forever.

"Switch on your TV," my friend said. She sounded frantic.

"What happened?"

"Gulshan, just put on the TV now. The news."

Our beloved doctor, the messiah of our newfound dreams, was arrested by the local police for running a fake Ayurvedic racket.

I was instantly hit with the drama and sensation that have now become an inherent part of the news narrative. The animated anchor was in his element and here I was too dazed to process the details. Apparently, 'the doctor' was mixing anti-epilepsy drugs along with the Ayurvedic medication.

Apart from the sudden shock, we were thrown right back into the whirlwind of panic. Zara was already on a certain dose of anti-epileptic medication, and here, we had no idea how much extra we were potentially pumping into her system.

Tears rolled down my cheeks as I pictured the flowers and diyas we had offered with such hope in our hearts.

Chapter 14

The Unanswered Question:
Why Me?

I was still not ready to give up. If anything, my ego became even more defiant. I am not sure if The Beatles got their answer in the holy land of Rishikesh, but I was meant to learn a lesson.

Friends began noticing my obsession with finding a cure for Zara. At first, they let it pass, probably thinking of it as a phase, but when they saw me unrelenting and going at it hammer and tongs, they intervened and asked me to stop. I promised on several occasions I would, but I was still in denial.

The truth was I was hurt, and only true acceptance would heal me. To accept that your child is not "normal" is hard, very hard. Especially at the stage of life when I saw normal as something very different from how I see it now. Normal and abnormal are two very loaded words. Not only did I fear how society would view my child, but equally how I would view her. To accept is to give up all expectation, to believe that who we are or what we have is okay. For me, at that stage, acceptance was giving up… losing.

"No, I am not stopping. There must be someone out there, someone who can relieve us of our pain," I said this to myself every few minutes.

I could not bear to go to another birthday party and watch another 'normal' child laughing and enjoying the growing years of their life while we sat in silence with the lights out, living from seizure to seizure.

I was always happy to hear from friends. However, invariably, in their excitement, they would begin giving me a lowdown of the various social activities, the overnight picnic outings. I'd be lying if I said it did not evoke a sense of envy and a passing shower of jealousy. It was heartwarming to learn that they genuinely missed our presence, but at the end of the day, it was us, it was ME that had to deal with all of this.

The unanswered question, "Why Me?" kept haunting me. I would not stop. Thousands of dirhams down the drain, there had to be light at the end of the tunnel. God cannot be this cruel.

This heady cocktail of hopelessness, pity, anger, victimhood, and an egoistic determination to prove the world wrong kept me going. This endless search brought us back a full circle to the city of our origin, Mumbai.

Our search would hopefully end here, I thought, the moment Zeheer, Jenai, and I found ourselves in an apartment in the western suburb of the city.

Chapter 15

Only Black

"Open your eyes. What do you see?" the self-styled hypnotist asked my husband.

"Nothing. Just the room."

"Look from your third eye. Now what do you see?"

"Only black."

The hypnotist did not get the answers he was looking for from my husband and turned to the small group around him.

"Aliens are coming to capture Zara!" he proclaimed dramatically.

"Come on quickly! Let us all huddle to protect her!"

"Look! It's Zylokane. He's coming. Quick!"

We all went into a huddle, fearful of even the sunlight streaming in through the window. We went into a panic; we had to protect Zara, who was not even present.

He handed us all a cone-shaped brass pendulum, which he said would ward off any alien invasion. He commanded us to remove any portraits in our home that had eyes on them, as aliens usually invaded from these eyes.

He also asked us to stop answering the phone, saying if we picked up when an alien was calling, it would spell disaster.

We left the place absolutely shaken but relieved that finally we had found something.

We took an auto-rickshaw to the nearest train station and were completely traumatised as we saw a group of transgender individuals surround our auto-rickshaw at the traffic signal. This is not new and happens routinely but given our state of mind and the aggressiveness with which this group was demanding money, we were petrified they could be the aliens in disguise, and we could take no chances. We paid them handsomely, much to their surprise, and delightfully, they left in a jiffy.

It did not end there. Every time the phone would ring, my older daughter Jenai would say, "Don't pick up; aliens could be calling."

The hypnotist had also handed us a piece of paper with a matrix-like design and a prayer which we had to recite in Zara's presence.

The veil of fantasy I was hiding behind was finally lifted. We realised that the matrix handed to us, which was supposed to perform miracles, was inspired by the Keanu Reeves superhit film *The Matrix*.

It was clear that all these misadventures had to stop and stop immediately. We were losing our money, our time, and most importantly, our minds. I knew I had no choice but to finally listen to the collective voices of sanity. My ego was hurt. It had been dying to show the medical fraternity that their opinion was not the be-all and end-all.

Ironically, in the crazy quest to cure Zara, I was no longer in touch with her. My connection to her was lost. I began sobbing as this realisation hit me. The fact that my older daughter's life had taken a back seat since Zara had consumed us was not lost on me. Every living moment of ours was spent countering, worrying, finding solace, a philosophy, a God, a quack, or just about anything that gave us even a glimmer of hope.

Desperation can be really ugly and depleting. I think even Zylokane would choose to leave us alone in this fatigued state.

My prayer table was like the shrine of the world. It had every kind of God people could possibly worship. My domestic help Rosie was proud of her contribution to this table. Zara had become extremely dear to her, and she too wanted to help.

Rosie began talking about an extremely famous pastor who was briefly visiting Dubai from Kerala, a state on the southern tip of India. His specialty was miracle healing, and she urged me to attend his mass healing programme at a prominent stadium. I told Rosie I was over all of this and had now 'accepted' our fate.

The mind, as we know, is a trap of sorts. It plays tricks on you when you least expect it. Could there be the smallest chance that Rosie's pastor could be the one? Just one more try…

Chapter 16

Connections

Man is a social animal. We've heard that over a hundred times. Our socialising has in it the comfort of familiarity.

It was the year 1999, and the World Wide Web (WWW) was the newest sensation in town. It had taken the world by storm and was arguably the biggest game-changer of the millennium. It all seemed very exciting back then, trying to understand this beast: dial-up connections, unpredictable internet speeds, and you were cooler than your friend if you signed up for Hotmail or Yahoo a little before them.

The new-age wizards, the creators of this web, were way ahead of the curve, not just in terms of understanding technology but also as amazing behavioural scientists.

Humans have forever initiated contact with each other, especially on long train rides, occasionally on airplanes, and in waiting areas of offices. There has always been something intriguing about initiating contact with a stranger, someone from another world who has nothing to do with us.

There is great comfort in familiarity, but there is an edgy curiosity about unfamiliarity. Unfamiliarity brings with it the excitement of unknown experiences and the relief of a temporary escape. How does it matter what a stranger thinks of you as opposed to the image you need to keep intact with all the familiar players? Many times we find ourselves yapping away, no holds barred, with a total stranger on a train, for we know fully well that come tomorrow, all will be forgotten, and we get back into our comfort zones.

I cannot recall the chat platform, but I am guessing it was the all-popular ICQ. ICQ was like a gigantic mall with multiple chat rooms based on country, area of interest, age, orientation, and a thousand other criteria to choose from. One could be as bold as one wanted or as adventurous as one dared to be, but to me, it was none of the above. It was just an escape and a genuine desire to connect with someone who was not a part of my everyday life and someone who did not relate to me as Zara's mother. After all these years, it was extremely difficult for people to relate to me as an individual. I was Zara's mother first, before anything else.

Laptops were unheard of back then, and we had a desktop just like everybody else. I would spend hours on several search engines trying to find out more about SMEI – Severe Myoclonic Epilepsy in Infancy, and by some stroke of chance, I happened to connect with a young boy who belonged to the Zoroastrian Parsi community, the same religious community that I belong to.

We barely got chatting, and we discovered we were both from Mumbai. He had just moved to England to study, and he really missed his home and his mother. He was mild-mannered and sensitive, and I enjoyed chatting with him. It was perfect- he was technically a stranger, but he did not feel strange at all. At best, this was an escape and, at worst, therapy, but it was working for both of us. He would feel less lonely talking with me, and I could share my situation with someone I didn't really know. He probably found in me the mother he was missing, and I found that non-judgemental friend with no connection with my life.

After conversing for months, he began researching Zara's illness and would pass on helpful links and send documents that he had compiled. We truly helped each other tide over our problems.

We had relocated to Dubai and similarly a lot of my close friends from Rustom Baug, the place I grew up in Mumbai had moved to different parts of the globe.

We were not the 'children of the internet'. A lot of us had moved away from each other's lives much before its advent and as a result had almost lost complete touch.

I was surprised and overwhelmed to see so many of my old friends taking a special interest in Zara's life. This also meant that I was swamped with a lot of good intentioned information I could not actually use as it was not pertinent to Zara's condition. The very fact that they would show so much concern and spend countless hours on research, taking time out of their busy lives is something that moves me till this day.

An old friend of Zeheer and myself went out of his way urging us to come to the USA. We would jointly find a way to find the required cure and also arrange funds.

Words like seizure and epilepsy had become buzzwords for me. I would be off like a bullet, pursuing the source, clinging onto a thin thread in the hope that somewhere, there'd be an answer.

Chapter 17

A Monkey Mind

The joy of a second child in the offing soon started replacing itself with a strange apprehension, a nagging at the back of the mind…a worry that this child may not be "normal." I was twenty-five when I had my first daughter Jenai. I was stronger and perhaps healthier. Now at the age of thirty-three, would this delivery be different? I kept trying to reason with myself, the mind as we know is always up to its tricks, a monkey mind.

Whatever I tried, this fear would creep back again and again. My premonition kept getting stronger. I decided to strike a deal with God. The terms of my deal were that if I had a normal child, I would devote substantial time to working with children with special needs. I promised over and over that I would take this deal very seriously.

The deal was signed and sealed, at least from my end. God only knows what the other party had in mind. I went on with my life, taking care of my home and spending time with my school-going daughter.

Days used to go by, and suddenly, the same fear would come rushing back. Logically, it made no sense. The feeling was stronger than ever. It would just not settle. In a fit of panic, I revoked the deal with God.

"God, give me a sick child. It's ok. I will handle it and accept it. This conversation appeared to have settled things. The recurring negative thinking was finally put to rest.

But the mind being a monkey was up to mischief again as the time for my delivery drew near. The worry to have a normal child again took over. Once again "Please, please!! Give me a healthy child. I will do anything you ask for."

As shameful as this might sound, the fact is we are more God-fearing than God-loving. I was no exception.

Chapter 18

A Taxi Ride

They call him the almighty for a reason. Cometh 5th of May 1997, there was my "normal" little baby girl. We would name her Zara. We would love her to the moon and back. I had it all covered. My older daughter would have a younger sibling, and we would be a picture-perfect family.

"Thank you, God! Time to fulfil my end of the bargain."

I decided I would become a volunteer and dedicate a part of my life to children with special needs.

The big question: where do I begin?

It was back in the 1990's that internet penetration was at its most nascent stage and finding anything off the net was not easy. On a whim, I thought I would get into a cab and see where it would take me. Let's try it unplanned.

My decision paid off. We often underestimate their intelligence, street smartness, their ability to hold the most interesting conversations and their wealth of life experience. They spend most of their lives on the roads and have seen it all; the cruel, the kind, the deceitful, the lovers, the elopers, the out and out criminals, the criminals in disguise, fear, death, compassion and the list goes on.

My particular driver belonged to the Pathan lineage and was a resident of Pakistan. I hopped into his cab and realised that communicating where I wanted to go was not going to be easy. I started by trying to be politically correct and asking him if he knew where I could find a school or any institution for children with special needs.

There was no way he was going to comprehend what I was trying to say. I cringed as I said "Aap ko koi aisi school ya sanstha ki jankari hai jaha wo bachhe jinka dimaag sahi nahi hai, aise bacche us school mein jaate hai?"

Translation to English: "Do you know of any school or institution where kids whose minds are backward or not right go? Retarded children?"

It saddened me that I had to use retarded or crazy to be understood. He knew what I was asking for, and I successfully found myself at the doorstep of DCSN – The Dubai Center for Special Needs.

I am convinced taxi drivers can be good therapists.

Chapter 19

I've Kept My Promise to You.

Finally! It's time for me to keep my word.

The moment was here. The realisation this is happening for real began sinking in as I inched closer to the building. It was the June of 1997 and six weeks post Zara's birth. I instinctively looked up to the heavens "God, I've kept my promise to you."

Dubai Center for Special Needs or DCSN as it is popularly known quickly became my home away from home. I experienced the unconditional love of over a hundred individuals with special needs, mostly children and a few adults. The staff was warm and welcoming. The coloured walls, the non-intimidating ambience were so comforting.

Reality sure can be stranger than fiction, but today, on my first day here, I was about to discover reality can also be scarier than fiction. A beautiful little girl suddenly gets a seizure, and her body begins to shiver and tremble, a sight I have never experienced at such close quarters. She was quickly taken away into another room. I immediately felt a sense of relief at the thought of not having to deal with the disturbing emotions that accompany an event of this nature.

I did not want to watch but I guess a hint of shame took over. I told myself I am here for a reason, and I cannot be so weak. This compelled me to reluctantly peek through the window into Alia's room, not sure if I wanted to come to terms with what had happened or to find comfort in the fact that it was over.

I learnt something about myself that day, and it baffled me. It is so easy to accept love, enjoy meeting people and be totally ok when everything is going well. Yet, I could barely stand the sight of the very girl who had just a moment ago showered me with love. We can only handle things that make us feel easy and comfortable. Ironically, we had no idea of how our own future with Zara would play out, and all I could think of was, "How can a mother handle all this? I am so glad I don't have to." This was only a month after Zara's birth, and there were absolutely no signs of her being anything other than a 'normal' healthy child.

My mind quickly galloped into a make-believe future; Zara would finish school, go to college, probably get married and start a family. A million fantasies, yet little do we know what our destiny holds in store for us.

Alia's seizure finally showed signs of subsiding, much like the highs and lows of life.

My tryst with special needs began with me being assigned a role in the art department. I would go on to assist Lorna Collaso who like me had spent most of her formative years growing up in Mumbai. We had both studied art in our hometown and were now thrown together for a common purpose.

My initial years were a truly humbling experience. I spent most of my time cutting, glueing and creating artwork. We had boards outside every classroom, as the centre had themes for which artwork needed to be created and glued onto the boards. We would have themes like the Eid festival, Christmas, and special days on which students and teachers undertook fun activities. On a lighter note, I suspect Lorna did not completely trust me with a larger role.

I also appointed myself as the official photographer and randomly went from class to class, capturing moments that could easily last several lifetimes with these special people. The impromptu photography sessions seemed to magically lift our collective spirits. It did the trick every time.

Birthdays at forty are expected to be hectic affairs where you throw a teeny-bopper style party, and all your 'adult' friends are expected to live it up to the hilt. I am only too glad mine turned out to be surprisingly different.

When we were in school, the class celebrated you with the happy birthday song but here the entire school celebrated. On my fortieth birthday, the faculty and students completely overwhelmed me with this surprise gesture. They specially organised a birthday assembly for me, lovingly and painstakingly made a large red banner with the words 'Happy Birthday Gulshan'. It means so much to me even today.

DCSN Dubai Center for Special Needs, where I spent 13 years and Zara was there for 10 years

Chapter 20

"If You Can't Find One, Start One."

And, just like that, it had been two years of volunteering at DCSN. By now, the severity of Zara's condition, our severely curbed social life, and the guilt of not being able to give my older daughter adequate attention were all taking a toll on me. I was severely sleep-deprived.

Denise, who was also a teacher at the centre, brought to my notice that I was beginning to slip into a depression. She was of the opinion that I should join a support group of sorts. We looked around for a support group for parents with special needs children, and we could not find a single one.

I faithfully 'reported' back to Denise. I guess depression was the way to go. I was too tired to think or fight with life anymore.

Denise looks me in the eye.

"If you can't find one, start one."

Did she just say that?

Here, I can barely stay awake, and she wants me to start a support group. Is she for real?

I could self-deprecate all I wanted, but deep down inside, Denise had said something of immense power.

Sandhya, my friend and Zara's volunteer, was sending her twin daughters to a special needs school by the name of Al-Noor. Ayesha Saeed was the practising psychologist at this special needs school. Ayesha had started a support group for a few children and their families, which was now in limbo. Sandhya felt that Ayesha might be the right person to team up with as she had previous experience with a support group.

Chapter 21

Meeting in My Living Room

Ayesha and I hit it off like a house on fire. The combination of shared geography and the strong underlying emotion that accompanies that geography had us hooked from the word go.

Ayesha was from Lucknow, the city of nawabs and coincidentally I was born and spent my childhood growing up in Lucknow where my mother's side of the family resided. When I think of it, I have met more people from different parts of India in Dubai than I would ever have actually met living in India.

Our meetings were full of nostalgia and reminiscence. We felt deeply connected.

9 December 1999 saw the humble beginnings of the Special Families Support Group (SFS). We started with six families meeting in my living room.

The meetings with other families made me realise that I was not the only one with a child who is differently abled, one with special needs. In fact, some of them had more than one member, up to four children, with some form of special needs.

Jenny and Sasha were a mother-and-daughter duo who frequented our group meetings. Jenny kept breaking down as handling her twenty-one-year-old daughter seemed impossible. Non-acceptance was a big part of the problem for most parents.

Jenny's daughter Sasha had Down syndrome. Unfortunately, the whole definition of what 'normal' is plays a huge part in the parents' psyche, leading to a non-acceptance of special needs. Special Needs are collectively and, to a large extent, falsely labelled as abnormal. It started to dawn on me that first, we would have to try and change this narrative for ourselves.

Jenny's plight made me realise this was not where I wanted to be emotionally and spiritually when Zara turned twenty-one. It was imperative that I align myself with this new normal.

As time passed, we realised that our numbers were not increasing. Most parents were still living in denial. Special Needs was not in their vocabulary and thinking. I decided to proactively go out interacting with families I found through contacts, references and randomly in shopping malls.

This was how I spotted Akeel, a young Sri Lankan boy and his mother at a popular supermarket. I was hesitant at first and knew I would be met with resistance, but my inner voice said, "Do it. It needs to be done." Akeel had been diagnosed with cerebral palsy coupled with blindness. It took many meetings to convince his mother that the support group would definitely help both Akeel and her. They finally joined and attended most of our weekly meetings. One day, Akeel's mother looked me in the eye and said, "There is hope. We are not alone, thank you."

Chapter 22

I Have a Daughter with Special Needs

In the summer of the year 2000, I happened to meet a woman at the reception of my daughter Zara's paediatrician. She was accompanying an eighteen-month-old boy who was unable to sit up on his own.

I introduced myself to her. The little boy was named Shivam.

"Shivam has Down Syndrome." I gently broke it to her.

"Who told you?" She shot back in denial.

"It's very obvious, especially when you look at his face."

"He's fine. We will show him to the doctor. We will go in for surgery if needed."

As guilty as I was for barging into their lives, I felt communicating with her was essential. Shivam's was a typical case of denial and non-acceptance. The roots of this lie in this societal idea of 'normal' and the parental fantasy of bringing up a child who would go on to become an 'achiever'.

It saddened me to know that a lot of children for whom we had started SFS were being denied an opportunity due to the close-mindedness of their parents. This resistance had to be effectively countered for us to make any headway.

I was aware we were running short on time, and she could be called in for her appointment anytime.

I went all guns blazing; shed light on my own experiences with Zara, the existence of an entity called the Special Needs group and how there is hope for both the family and the individual with special Needs.

As anticipated, it was time for her to meet with the paediatrician, and as she left my sight, I could only hope that our brief interaction would bring about a shift in mindset.

Shivam's family became the latest entrant to the growing SFS family.

Today, Shivam is a grown man living his life fully and being loved with total acceptance of his condition. He has successfully completed a course in Hotel Management and has briefly worked at a leading hospitality chain. He is currently at the Shaurya Foundation in India, which specialises in educating people with special needs and helping them to be self-sufficient in the future.

Every month at SFS we would have a party. It was just to be in the moment, share a few laughs and dance to our favourite songs.

"Why aren't you dancing? Come, let's have a little fun," I would coax especially the new members to join in the fun.

"Easy for you to say," one of them retorted sharply.

"You don't have a child with special needs."

These words took me by surprise. It dawned on me that a lot of the parents, mostly the new ones who did not know me, felt I was the chief volunteer, the proverbial 'outsider' looking to help the community.

I had always thought, up until that point at least, that Zara was the reason I was doing all of this. To me, this was the only logic that made sense. A few months down the road, I realised that SFS was not about Zara or me. SFS, for me, became bigger and more important than just my personal situation.

"I have a daughter with special needs" I gently broke it to them.

The connection was instant. The game had changed. Parents now wanted to take ownership of their children as they started to accept their situation.

SFS parties over the years

Chapter 23

500 Families

---

9 December 2000 came in a jiffy. The calendar had flipped a whole 365 days. It seemed hard to fathom that just a year ago, Ayesha and I had started out with six families. I allowed myself an indulgent smile at the fleeting memory of our humble beginning, a handful of people in my living room. On that day, a year later, on our first anniversary, there were 200 people. We called it the Special Families Support Group. It popularly came to be known by the acronym SFS.

If this was a start-up, we certainly would have had investor interest, I thought to myself jokingly. On the contrary, this was anything but an enterprise flushed with funds. A self-help group was kept alive because of shared circumstances. This was our first anniversary, and I could not let the lack of a budget get in the way of a celebration we all deserved.

The hotel apartment where I was living agreed to let us use their beautiful outdoor park free of cost. This came as a big relief as we now had a venue.

In time, we managed to get sponsors who were moved by our cause. We got a company to construct a ramp, an apparel retailer provided the clothes, and a DJ gave us his services, again free of cost. The kids had a great time on the stage, and so did all the parents and volunteers. I was touched that so many professionals from different walks of life came forward to help make this happen.

It is worth mentioning here that all this was happening in the pre-WhatsApp era. Each parent involved had to be contacted by phone. I started making my share of calls inviting them, but what invariably happened was that they would spend hours talking about their challenges. It was exhausting, but it was worth every minute.

Today, in the year 2024, we have approximately 500 families.

Another memory was that of our first summer camp at my dear friend Jeroo's large house and garden.

It all started one afternoon when I found myself at a lunch where a well-known public figure from India had invited people to fundraise. Dubai was by then a melting pot of cultures, and I had been witness to the metamorphosis it had undergone in terms of outlook. This prosperous emirate slowly transformed itself from just wealth creation to value creation, especially in terms of supporting worthy causes. The primary reason I attribute this is that its citizenry, thanks to global connectivity, has become far more aware as a people and as a collective.

We were all asked to present our propositions one by one about how we wished to contribute to the community.

Among the many things, I also expressed my request about the Special Families Support (SFS) looking for a large space to host their first summer camp.

"You can use my house." Jeroo unhesitatingly jumped in with this offer.

I had half a mind to ask her, "Are you sure"? Given the spontaneity of the decision. However, I decided to unquestionably accept that day as our lucky day.

Jeroo's beautifully done-up home had a variety of curios. I instantly began picking them up and putting them away in case they broke.

"Why are you clearing them out? Leave them there!"

"What if they break?"

"Let them. If they're meant to break, they will."

I was deeply touched. The kids being there was more important to Jeroo than her expensive curios. That made it even more special.

Many young children, my older daughter's friends, came forward to volunteer. It was a landmark moment of sorts. For the first time, the lines between normal and not normal began to blur as these youngsters embraced each other wholeheartedly.

The children with special needs and the other children came closer. I saw it unfold before my very eyes – it was an eye-opener for the other children that children with special needs weren't really that different; they were just 'special'.

There was fun, love, interaction and a lifetime of growth for both sets of children. This is how change begins I suppose, when the 'normal' begin to truly accept the 'special'.

"Money makes the world go round." we often hear this phrase. To a large extent, I believed this to be true up until this point. From my experience, I can say that when people believe they can touch another life deeply, they can truly give of themselves. The purpose and the meaning this gives their lives, far exceeds the allure of money. Funnily, in our materialistic world we often forget this.

"Money doesn't make the world go round; purpose and meaning do. Money has its place as a valuable medium."

Jeroo and Bali opened their home and hearts to SFS

Chapter 24

A Camera Called Nilofar

Nilofar, to me, is the most beautiful girl in the world. Her mother, Hanifa, is the epitome of courage to me.

Over the years be it the volunteering at the Dubai Center for Special Needs or creating value for our SFS group, I had accepted that if we had to make this work, I would need to be the prime motivator. I would need to keep doing this irrespective of the ups and downs in my life. I was also acutely aware this would be in addition to the inevitable stress and strain of being a mother to a child with special needs.

The good thing was that this helped me to forget about me; the bad thing was that it helped me to forget about me.

Media groups in the Middle East and a few television channels of Indian origin showed interest in covering us. Media publicity is always a great thing for a cause like this. Special Needs without the correct awareness is either met with awkwardness, indifference or considered plain backward or retarded. Today, I can proudly claim that, at least in Dubai, we are comparatively better off in terms of awareness and a mental shift. Back then, even the term 'special needs' was alien to most.

I had heard somewhere that if a majority of the population was faced with two choices, the first one to speak in public and the second one to face death, most would choose the latter. I found this absurd until I heard a journalist ask me to speak to the camera on the occasion of SFS's first anniversary. I found my hands getting clammy and my shoulders stiffening at the very thought. No, I cannot do this. I certainly did not want to die either, but I was happy not getting publicity for myself.

Nilofar, a young child with special needs who was also suffering from alopecia (the condition where you get no growth of hair anywhere on the body), to my surprise, noticed my nervousness.

"Talking to a camera is like talking to a person."

She took the mike from the journalist's hand and handed it over to me. She then stood right next to the camera.

"Forget you are talking to many people. If you stare at the camera, you will get nervous. Look at me and think you are talking to me."

A girl with special needs had the maturity and the emotional intelligence to understand exactly what I needed.

Moments later, I was looking at this 'camera' named Nilofar.

She literally became my lens to the world by just shifting my perspective. People pay big money to learn the art of public speaking, and here I was, talking away unhesitatingly, as I have done to date. I have not looked back since.

Countless parents, through the years of being associated with SFS, have told me that they don't feel alone anymore. I, too, stopped feeling alone as SFS developed and gained an identity of its own.

In 2010, Nilofar's mother, Hanifa, called me with the bad news that her husband had suddenly passed away. Nilofar and her brother Nadeem, also an individual with special needs, were permitted to live in the Middle East only on her husband's visa sponsorship.

"Gulshan, please somehow see to it that my children and I don't have to leave the country." was her only plea to me.

Hanifa, who had never worked a day in her life and did not know how to operate an ATM machine, managed to get herself a job in a school for children with special needs called Manzil. With sheer grit and determination, she managed to keep her children in Dubai.

Incidents like this made me appreciate my privilege. I had a wonderfully supportive husband and older daughter. We had the financial means to take care of Zara. Hanifa's heart wrenching story made me see life in a different light.

Hanifa had two such children. I have met families where up to four children needed special needs care.

Hanifa and many such individuals like her have reinforced my faith that we created SFS for the right reasons. It has, in fact, become the elixir of hope for so many families in distress.

Chapter 25

Make That Call, Do That Visit

At SFS, we tried our best to support families emotionally, spiritually, and of course, financially.

Children with special needs need to go to special schools that are pretty expensive. The average annual fees of schools were about 50,000 dirhams. In addition, medical expenses had to be taken care of, which could run up to exorbitant amounts.

If we did not do something about this, a vicious cycle of emotional and spiritual brokenness would take over. I decided to start contacting corporates, high net worth individuals, insurance companies and whoever else I could think of to help us financially.

There was a downside to this. The families quickly got dependent on SFS's help and simply did not have the will or the confidence to help themselves. This, I realised, was financially and emotionally unsustainable. My team and I started to gradually encourage each family to take matters into their own hands. Our constant motivational reminders to them were, "Make that call, do that visit. Speak up for yourself. Ask for what you need."

Many families got some form of help or the other, be it in in the form of school fees or medical expenses.

Another issue cropped up - many families had one 'normal' child and one child with special needs. They decided it was best to spend their limited budget on educating the 'normal' child and were not interested in spending on the education of the other child.

"What is the use? They can never marry and get a job."

Despite all the progress we had made at SFS and through the media, I realised we still had our work cut out for us. Many of the families had still not realised that with the proper training and care a lot of the children with special needs can be transformed into extremely capable individuals. In some instances, like Shivam and Nilofar, even rub shoulders with their 'normal' counter parts.

Shivam, the little boy who could not sit up at eighteen months of age, diagnosed with down syndrome, today works for a hospitality chain in India. He is an independent person earning and contributing.

Nilofar works for a bank in Dubai and gets a yearly increment as a reward for good work. She is known for her punctuality, is conscientious and well-loved by her colleagues.

Shivam and Nilofar are shining examples of what timely intervention and instilling awareness by way of effective training can do for individuals with special needs. It is my hope and dream that every individual is as blessed, for there are still too many who are languishing as they have never been trained to be self-dependent and self-reliant.

As satisfying as the journey has been, in the quiet of the night when I am alone and when Zara gets her millionth seizure, I lose hope and want to run away, escape it all.

My mind goes back to that big white blank canvas I had in my art class. That canvas depicts life. Life is blank, then you create something, and a cause and effect takes place.

I would use the same analogy with my students. The blank white canvas stares them in the face. They are equipped with a variety of paints and a good paintbrush.

"Don't just start painting. Ask yourself what you want in your life?"

They'd stare back blankly, and I'd clarify, "Not your whole life. Can you just imagine the next step?"

"What colour do you want to choose? Think about what you want to create. One step at a time."

You start believing in them, and they start believing in themselves.

One person must believe. I decided I would be that one person.

I felt at peace with my truth.

Rekha ideating on her blank canvas, working... and then at her exhibition

Chapter 26

My Saviour

One afternoon, during our formative years at SFS, my dear friend Sandhya introduced us to Saif Bijliwala, an occupational therapist from Mumbai.

Saif was exactly what the ecosystem needed at this time. He had conducted a rather insightful session on what children with special needs actually need and the attitudinal shift parents would need to make in order to have a better quality of life given the situation.

A lot of families attended his session. The Q & A leg of the session was what I found fascinating. It gave me a deeper insight on what was happening with the kids, their challenges, their trials, and the different forms of individual struggle that parents were facing.

"Our child has no patience. We have a particularly hard time when we are flying. The entire experience is a nightmare as he just won't sit still."

Saif simplified this in a second "Stop picking and dropping your children by car. Stop pampering them."

He was quick to gauge this was a problem most parents were facing.

"Let your child get used to waiting at the bus stop. Let them get into this routine, and over time, you will see how much patience they develop. Do this, and you won't need to ask the airline for special privileges."

The audience was hooked. The overprotective parent was told they need to let their child experience life as routinely and as normally as possible. A shift in thought led to life changing experiences for both parents and kids.

"Stop spoiling them. Let them learn to wait patiently" He emphasised this repeatedly.

I realised at SFS we were advising and assisting a lot of parents to learn how to cope. Our understanding was that we were merely trying to do our best in a hopeless situation. Saif made us all realise this was not true.

Adopting his techniques helped tremendously. Some children learnt to take public transport on their own, do groceries, behave well at airports and the results were there to see—they were less anxious and went about navigating life situations better.

On the personal front, my younger daughter Zara was now three years old. She had regressed to the point where she had stopped walking. I decided it was time to get Saif to intervene and help her with intensive sessions.

He had his ways. Five minutes into the very first session, Saif almost lifted Zara by her fingers and made her stand up on her feet. My heart skipped a beat as I watched her manage to gingerly stay on her feet.

I desperately wanted to control this situation. I wanted to tell Saif to go easy on her. I cannot remember the last time Zara was on her feet. He turned her around in circles, almost like he was attempting to jive with her. I felt like he was reading my mind and choosing to do the exact opposite. I quickly reminded myself of the reason I wanted him to work with Zara in the first place. I let the mother in me rest.

"Stop! My granddaughter has epilepsy."

My mother, who had flown down from Mumbai to be with us, decided enough was enough.

"It's ok. She will get a seizure," Saif replied nonchalantly.

This man either knew exactly what he was doing, or he was plain crazy.

Now, it seemed like it was my mother's turn to read my mind and do exactly the opposite.

"Ai, ghelo ne gher thi bhar kar," she rattles off in Gujarati, our mother tongue.

"Take this madman out of the house," she urges me.

"Ma, he knows Gujrati." I inform her.

This was just brilliant. Saif now knew he was a madman, at least where my family was concerned, and it seemed not to bother him in the least.

This 'madman' knew exactly what he was doing. Saif came over three to four times a week and soon Zara was walking without any help. In a span of three to four years she was walking up and down the stairs. He taught her to eat by herself and she was trained to pour water from a jug which was always kept at the same place.

Sadly, a lot of the good work he did with her got completely erased from Zara's memory when she suffered a cluster of seizures in a very short period. Interestingly, despite all of this, she never forgot how to walk, but surprisingly, she forgot how to eat by herself and could not recall the pouring of water from the jug. She stopped doing that for herself.

Saif patiently taught and re-taught her these skills over a hundred times. He is one of the most patient teachers I know.

I have huge respect for this man. An occupational therapist by profession, he became our saviour. Zara learnt how to walk again.

He opened our eyes to how much an individual with special needs can progress despite the regression. Zara had regressed to lying in a corner all day before Saif came into her life.

He decided to go back to India to his clinic after his stint in Dubai for several years. During his time here, he helped several parents at SFS who could not afford to pay his fees. He was instrumental in ensuring hundreds of children with special needs learnt to stand and walk when all hope was lost.

To this day whenever I am in Mumbai, Zara goes over to Saif's clinic to learn some skill or the other.

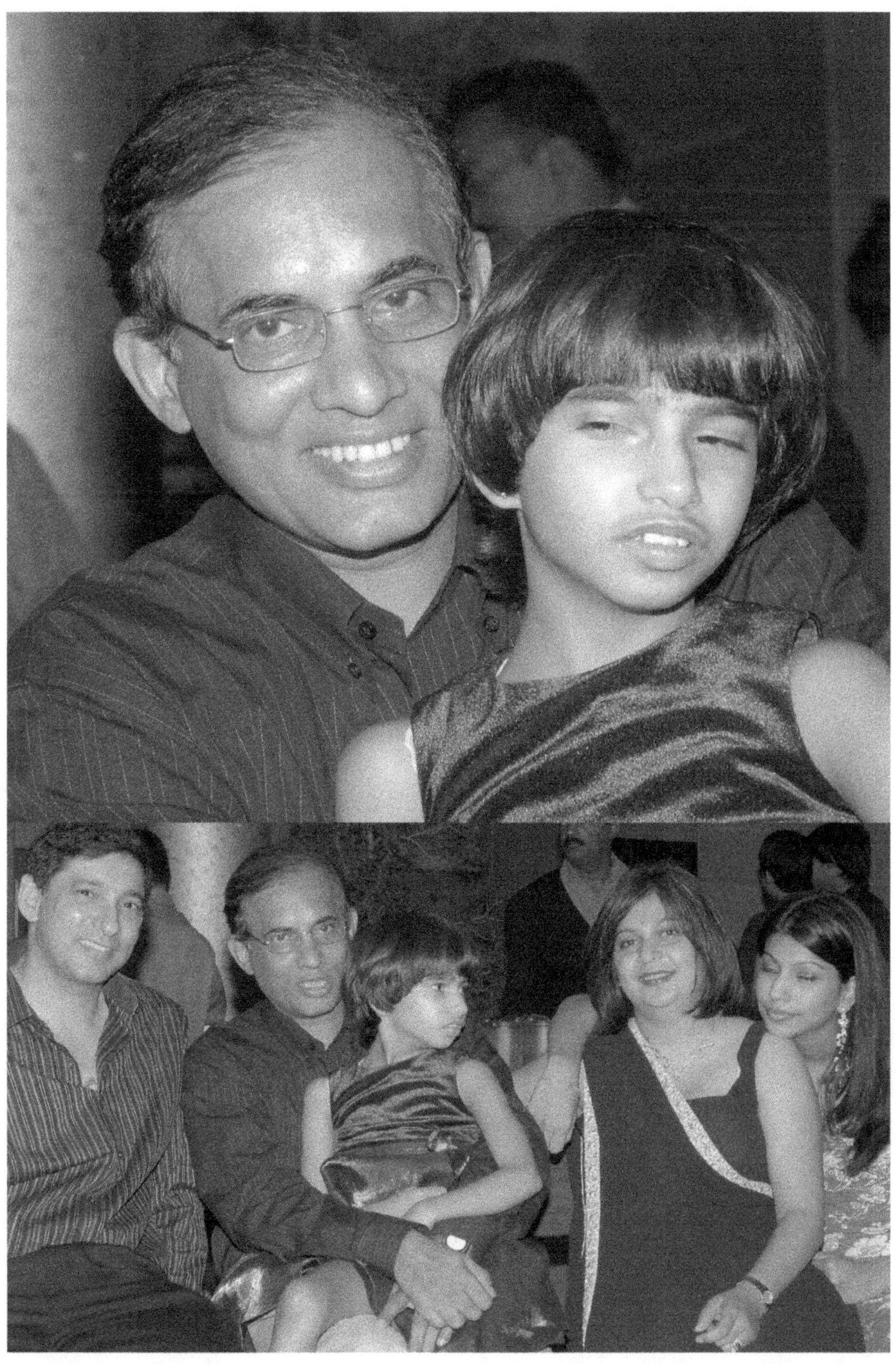

Saif, our saviour

Chapter 27

Flower Girl

Saif was the first angel I was introduced to by Sandhya, my dear departed friend.

Shortly after Saif had entered our lives, Sandhya introduced us to Vanessa Sequeira, who was training to become a special needs educator and caregiver. Her special interest was autism, and she wanted to apply her training to help Zara. Vanessa would often come just to observe Saif working with Zara.

She would employ therapies like wrapping Zara in a towel and rolling an exercise ball over her, exerting enough pressure in an attempt to stimulate the nerves. She would give Zara sensory therapy exposing her to hot and cold stimuli.

After two years of relentlessly working with Zara, Vanessa broke down.

"I don't think I'm doing anything right."

Vanessa felt that Zara was not responding to any form of therapy, and self-doubt had begun to creep in.

Vanessa would often sing to Zara, and Zara would smile back in acknowledgement.

"Vanessa, something is happening. Something is definitely happening," I used to assure her.

We travelled to Sri Lanka for the joyous occasion of Vanessa's wedding. We would not miss this for the world. It was the year the tsunami had wreaked havoc there. She wanted Zara to be her flower girl. I was choked with emotion. Zara had never been made to feel this special.

Zara made a beautiful and very special flower girl. My older daughter Jenai played "Here Comes the Bride" on the guitar.

Zara ended up having a bad seizure right after. The exertion had been just too much for her, but I thought to myself, what the hell? She was made to feel so wanted. We took Zara to a quiet corner, knowing that had Vanessa to witness any of this, She would have been extremely upset. Vanessa had been just an intrinsic part of Zara's life, and today was her day. I could not let even the worst seizure come in the way.

Zara became a regular invitee to Vanessa's special Christmas family get togethers. Vanessa would cook the food Zara liked, some special chicken dishes. Vanessa had become an intrinsic part of Zara's life and for us, she was more like family.

One day, Vanessa asked us if she could take Zara home to spend the day with her family.

Despite the love and care Vanessa showered for Zara; we still had trust issues. Over the years, given our experience with Zara's sudden and unpredictable seizures, we felt no one but us, the immediate family, could handle her at times like these. This was a big decision for us.

But Vanessa was persistent, and we could see she really wanted to do this. We finally relented.

We dropped Zara off at Vanessa's home but kept driving around the block, expecting to be called any time.

To our surprise, the call never came. After a few hours of endlessly circling around the block, it was time to pick her up.

Vanessa opened the door and saw Zara sitting on a tiny stool. There was vomit on Vanessa's father; her brother came into the room, and there was vomit on him, too! In their love, they had totally overfed her, and she threw up on everyone.

Cut to 2005: Jenai, my older daughter was about to turn sixteen. We had never taken a family holiday together. Frankly the thought of taking one had never crossed our minds.

We had recently won two tickets to London, and we wanted to travel a lot. But how?

Vanessa and my domestic help from India, Rosie, stepped up to the task. It was the first time in eight years that Zara would be spending a full ten days without either Zeheer, Jenai or me.

The initial days of our trip, right after leaving the shores of Dubai, were filled with apprehension and anxiety. At any given a chance, we kept calling to find out how Zara was.

"She's fine. She's well," their standard reply to our barrage of questions.

"Did she get a seizure?" was our question on every call, every day, several times a day.

"She is absolutely fine," much to our relief.

It took days before we started to enjoy London.

We would later discover that Zara did have a few seizures in our absence, but both Rosie and Vanessa decided that they would not worry us, come what may.

Zara has made me experience love in ways I would have never known otherwise. I am ever so grateful to Vanessa for persisting with Zara over the years. She took care of Zara like a parent and made her a part of her family. Can one expect more?

Chapter 28

"If It Bothers You,
Look the Other Way."

My world gradually began opening up. I connected with many wonderful people. I would teach, volunteer, help raise awareness, and secure finances for the special needs community. This was now my life.

Over time Jeroo became my go to friend; 4 am, 4 pm and all the hours in between.

She would often jump into her car and be at my place in a jiffy. Just to be there.

We would just sit in silence. We had no way of stopping the seizure.

"I am sorry, I can't help. All I can do is be there for you."

This is all I really needed. Her presence and her being there.

In our moments of silence, my mind would often wander back in time to those moments where I chose to offer unsolicited advice when all someone wanted was perhaps my presence.

I cannot help but think about my first interaction with Jeroo at the fundraising event.

"Can you please not smoke?"

"If it bothers you, look the other way."

This woman, who I had ridiculed based on a first impression, became my support and strength.

She would sit there holding Zara, patting her back lovingly.

In times of crisis, the first person I call is Jeroo after I call my husband. Always, to this day.

Me, Johaan and Jeroo

Chapter 29

"I Know What You're Going Through"

We often talk of sibling rivalry. Roxane and I have had our fair share, but she is a loving older sister who has stood by me unconditionally. Roxane feels my pain first-hand. Her younger daughter Alysha is Zara's age.

As young parents we are obsessed with our children doing well and consistently achieving some preconceived milestones. I had no idea how much I had bought into society's idea of the 'ideal' growth of a child. When Zara was born, I had dreams for her- What kind of student would she be? A class topper, or more creatively inclined like my older daughter and myself? Where would she pursue her higher studies? When would she choose to get married? Would I play with her children someday?

When I think back on what the pain of the non-acceptance of our situation did to us, it makes me firmly believe that we need to reassess our concept of "normal "and "abnormal." What really is normal? I have come to experience that beauty lies in all things: the so-called normal and abnormal, the similar and the different. I arrived at this conclusion after working with and spending a whole part of my life with individuals with special needs. If we look at them through the prism of understanding and empathy, these individuals are truly special. They bring with them unique characteristics and make you see the beauty of this world – only they can do this.

Alysha was such an effervescent child. Intelligent, charming and would entertain us with her dancing and singing skills.

As much as I love Alysha, it was too close to home not to compare her 'progress' to that of Zara, especially given they are of the same age. Not just Alysha, it became difficult for me to compare Zara with any others.

Roxane deeply understood this and would always make herself available. Like Jeroo in Dubai, Roxane would never dole out unsolicited advice. She realised quickly that all I needed was her presence, her understanding and her willingness to be there for me.

Much against her will, just for me, she, and her husband Behram had attended a séance session. I was told that the right spirit would have an answer to Zara's problems.

Roxane and Behram attended one such session and sat in a dark room where, gradually, the medium's voice changed from a female voice to a male voice. Believe me, had Roxane asked me to do the same for her, I would have been petrified and would have flatly refused.

"Someone in this room is blocking the energy."

My sister and brother-in-law were told in a room full of people that they needed to leave the room as they were the ones blocking the energy.

Roxane never once complained to me or judged my unreasonable demands.

She has visited many such places at my behest. Roxane went through it all unquestioningly.

She often bore the brunt of my anger.

"I know what you're going through" she would say

"The hell, you know. You don't know," I'd shoot back in anger.

My sister often became my punching bag. She helped me through my worst times. The love she has for me I treasure like no other. I thank her for being there for me when I was as crazy as can be.

Top: *Roxane, my mum Perin and I* | **Bottom:** *Me with my mum Perin and mother-in-law, Aran*

My sister, Roxane and my sister-in-law Purnoor - my support systems

Chapter 30

The Wind Beneath My Wings

In the initial years, I would stay up night after night with Zara. Zeheer had a full-time job, and I did this to give him undisturbed sleep. The only way Zara would sleep was if I held her in my arms. My arms ached and ached over time. The pain would get unbearable. I did this day after day, night after night. I had made her my responsibility. I did not share my pain with Zeheer. I developed gall bladder problems and a hernia, underwent numerous surgeries, and, over time, developed a sleeping disorder.

Zara had just turned ten and it became obvious to Zeheer that with each passing year, it would get harder for me to handle her physically. He quietly took over. She weighed thirty kilos, and he would caringly carry her, change her diapers in the middle of the night. All this without saying a word or making a fuss.

The trickiest bit was her medication. It had to be systematically done, specific timings, varying doses and close follow-ups with doctors for changes in medication and dosage. Sometimes the dosage would change every few weeks according to her change in weight. It meant that her weight had to be monitored for even minute fluctuations. Zeheer took charge of all this completely. I marvel as to how he did all of this without once showing the slightest bit of anger or frustration. I still have a lot to learn from him.

Zeheer never questioned or criticised me when I'd drag him through all our countless, fruitless endeavours to find a cure. I guess we were both willing to do anything to cure Zara. In a way, I think he had an inner acceptance that I continued to struggle with.

"Whatever you want, we'll do," Zeheer had once told me, and whatever I wanted, we did.

He gave me unconditional support in all my volunteer work.

A lot of people, even those who know me well, often forget that I have a child with special needs. There was a time when Zara would have up to seven seizures a day.

"Leave her with me, and don't worry. You go to SFS."

Zeheer truly understood the value of SFS and never once felt I was ignoring Zara. He also knew that if I had to choose, I would choose Zara, and he never let it come to that.

I would finish my day at SFS and only later would get to know that Zara had a seizure, and Zeheer did not tell me. He took complete care of her. Once again, quietly.

His presence at our SFS meetings transformed a whole lot of people. He never intended to be an influencer, a change agent, or a catalyst, yet he was all of that and more.

Zeheer would feed Zara at SFS as he would normally do at home. We did not realise that such a routine act would become the topic of discussion among the men folk. Other fathers slowly started imbibing this. Many fathers started feeding their kids.

Zeheer did this not with the intention to change anyone else; not once did he pass judgement or think he was doing anything special. He simply did it because he cared.

He also ensured that he gave equal time to both his daughters. He would often just spend time listening to Jenai playing her songs on the guitar. He never missed a single parent teacher meeting. Many times, he did not actually understand why Jenai or I wanted to do something, but he would just be there with us and participate.

Once he had accepted the situation, his acceptance was total. Mine wavered ever so often.

He is firmly rooted in reality. I have broken down several times. Zeheer had dedicated himself to her. She was totally a part of him.

People think of me as the strong one, but it is he who is the stronger. He truly is the wind beneath my wings.

I am vocal and emphatic. He does it all silently.

My pillar of strength

Chapter 31

Spotlight

I often reflect on the utter helplessness and loneliness I had felt during the initial years; but it is now short lived. Today I feel the contentment that comes from having touched the lives of countless individuals and families through the Dubai Center for Special Needs (DCSN) and our efforts at SFS.

It all started with a personal need and has expanded into something of real value.

I went about my work with a passion and a sense of purpose. One afternoon, I was pleasantly surprised to find an email stating that I was one of the nominees of the Princess Haya award for the most outstanding special needs family. The prize money for the winner would be AED 25,000. This award was reserved for only those families who were currently raising a special needs child of their own and had contributed to the special needs community at large.

Special needs awareness has indeed come a long way.

I had never looked at any of this as my contribution or for that matter, as an achievement and yet I was being acknowledged. I loved my little hall of fame moment. I excitedly submitted a report to the organisers highlighting my work at DCSN and SFS though the years 1998-2008.

The first person I decided to call with the good news was my mother.

"It's good, but you're only successful if you make money."

The excitement that I was feeling came crashing down.

'Could she be right?' It was hard to accept that all my initiatives had no value because this was not earning me any money. Is this the truth? I began doubting myself.

My anger at this motherly barb slowly gave way to realising that she had come from another world. She had yet to realise what setting up SFS meant to me and how it had transformed me in a way nothing else could. Today, my mother is not around. I wish I could share this time with her; I am invited all over the world to present the achievements of SFS and my special needs art students.

We were invited to attend the first edition of the Princess Haya Award at the ballroom of the Madinat Hotel, Dubai. We were sharing the table with an Emirati family, the original residents of Dubai. All of a sudden, a spotlight shone on our table, bringing us into sharp focus. Apparently, both families, mine and the ones we shared the table with, were declared joint winners of this award.

Later that year, I was approached by Wemmy DeMaaker, who was passionate about helping not only children but also adults with special needs.

Wemmy wanted to create an art studio where individuals would learn life skills through art. I was instantly excited at the idea. Art was my lifeline.

Wemmy wanted me to volunteer, and my response would have been a categorical "yes" had it not been for my dear departed mother's words: "It's good, but you're only successful if you make money."

"Wemmy, I will join you but not as a volunteer. I will join as a paid employee."

I was hesitant as I had, to date, never ever asked anyone for a paid job.

Wemmy agreed, and thanks to my mother, I landed my first paid job at the age of forty-six in 2010.

Celebrating my 50th birthday with my students at Mawaheb

Chapter 32

Mawaheb

It took a full two years after our first meeting for Wemmy to get the entire set-up going from construction to completion.

The art studio finally opened in 2010 and we were to start a journey that has been life changing for me and several other people.

It was called Mawaheb, which means talent in Arabic. Mawaheb took its baby steps and began working with adults who had disabilities. The idea was to use art as therapy. I was incredibly nervous as it was my first job at the age of forty-six. I felt like a student just out of art school.

I was filled with gratitude that I happened to be here, in Dubai, at this chosen moment. An arid land a few decades ago was transforming in so many ways. Mawaheb was a prime example of that paradigm shift.

Zara was now thirteen years old, and I could not help but look back at my conversations with God a few years ago.

"Why Me?"

Zara's thirteen years had created such an opportunity that from constantly asking God, "Why Me?" something had definitely stirred a feeling within me. I often began saying, "Why Not Me?" Admittedly, there were bad days, but then a sliver of gratitude would manage to find its way. I would often smile to myself, "Thank God, ME!."

It so happened that most of the students were individuals I was familiar with back from The DCSN and from our support group SFS.

Every day at Mawaheb was as much of a learning for me as it was for my students. We were here to grow through art, and there was absolutely no doubt in my mind that we would achieve something beautiful and rewarding together. Expressing oneself through art gives an individual the liberty to truly find themselves. I knew that I had to first encourage them to simply express themselves through strokes, colours, blacks and whites. Express their joys, anger, rage, and frustration. Just put it out there.

When an opportunity is given, it is amazing how the heart and mind opens up. I loved the magical creativity that was depicted on canvas.

I wanted them to learn to express themselves and also to be responsible adults. They loved the art class but would loathe the cleaning-up process that followed right after. I decided nobody could leave for the day till they responsibly put lids on all the paint bottles, put coloured pencils back in their cases and washed their brushes. Responsibility had to slowly be instilled. It is amazing how quickly they learnt to function as responsible adults. Of course, the occasional outbursts and odd tantrums had to be dealt with, too.

"You cannot behave this way. Please go out of class, change your mood and then come back."

Compassion and firmness often go together.

I deliberately created an almost zero-tolerance policy towards mood swings, exhibiting frustration or any form of tantrum throwing. A lot of them had never experienced this kind of empathy or firmness.

I had worked with most of these individuals earlier, but Mawaheb was the opportunity given to us to collectively try and improve adult interpersonal skills and behaviour, using art as the premise and the medium to transform. At Mawaheb, we also had a lot of people visiting us. Volunteers wanted to work alongside our artists. We had exhibitions where people could buy our paintings. They now had to interact with people they were not familiar with. This was a huge learning too.

These were individuals with disabilities, but they were adults too. I treated them so, and in turn they too started behaving as more responsible adults.

Mawaheb was more than just an art school. It had given me the unique opportunity of changing the way the 'normal' world viewed individuals with special needs and other disabilities.

Chapter 33

Normal with a Difference

Judy Singer, an autistic Australian sociologist, in the year 1998 coined the word "neurodivergent" to basically explain the concept of neurodiversity. Judy Singer and many others have worked so hard to give neurodiversity the respect it deserves: "I would ideally like the world to slowly begin looking at individuals with special needs as simply 'normal with a difference' and not disability."

The recognition of neurodiversity has proved to be path-breaking, and today, we attribute a lot of the attitudinal changes to how 'normal' or 'neurotypical' individuals view 'neurodivergent' folk or people with disability.

Judy Singer by coining the term encouraged other stakeholders to begin probing and researching further into the neurological differences between neurodiverse and neurotypical individuals. A significant volume of work has been done in the three decades since we first heard the term. Today we regard neurodiverse people as having a differently wired brain to others.

In this context, the Mawaheb opportunity was far bigger than I had envisioned. I felt Mawaheb had a mission. Firstly, to help people use art as therapy and more importantly to make them realise they were like normal people with a difference. Ultimately for larger society to realise this too. Once the artists gained confidence in themselves, Mawaheb encouraged them to have careers.

The Mawaheb dynamic was different from the Dubai Centre for Special Needs or from our Special Needs Support group in that, along with the elements of nurture, care and attention that all three institutions had in common, Mawaheb took it a step higher and nurtured artistic talent and had the ability to give these special needs artists' careers. These weren't artists who were being asked to rustle up a painting or two by their indulgent loved ones. This was business. Some of our most celebrated artists are world-renowned figures today.

These artists have never had an opportunity to rub shoulders with corporate houses, art galleries and other professionals. Mawaheb gave them this opportunity.

Chapter 34

It's Not Acceptable

Mawaheb had individuals who had varying degrees of ability. If a true sense of inclusion had to be nurtured, it would need an openness on our part to really understand each one's ability and disability. Mawaheb was just that; through the medium of an art school, we taught life lessons. Volunteers were instructed on how to be as inclusive as possible. Independence of thought was always encouraged. How to present oneself in front of prospective buyers and how to explain what their art stood for was something we slowly worked towards. It was an attempt at making each one realise their sense of self. It was a lot of work, but we were determined that Mawaheb would be a place where they not only felt comfortable, learnt the art and other interpersonal skills, but also realised their potential as worthy adults.

Victor Sitali, a 21-year-old young man from Zambia and audibly challenged was one of our most talented artists. I had known him from when he was 16 years old from my long stint as a volunteer with the Dubai Center of Special Needs. Victor's mother dropped him off every morning and I noticed that he was late every single day.

"You need to start coming on time. If you are at an office, would this be acceptable?"

Victor had no idea as he'd never worked in his life. He stared back blankly.

"No, it wouldn't. It is not acceptable."

I schooled Victor and his mother on how the real-world works. I made it clear to his mother that just because Victor had a disability, we could not use that as an excuse for indiscipline. It was imperative that she as his mother made him aware of the value of punctuality.

Getting through to Victor was important, and if I were to make this work, I had to learn ASL and American Sign Language. I put in the needed hours, and finally, Victor had someone outside his family to whom he could understand and talk.

Victor and his mother cited traffic as a problem. I asked him to use the metro service. Dubai has a very efficient metro rail service. I managed to convince both him and his mother that he would be safe by himself.

"Ma'am, your son is lost."

I get a phone call from the metro rail authorities. I instantly knew they were referring to Victor. He had missed all the stops and was now on the last stop, way off his destination.

I was in half a mind to go pick him. I instead requested the security man to put him on the next train back. Victor made his way back, never got lost again. He also started coming to Mawaheb on time.

After Victor, twenty-five out of our twenty-seven students started using the metro. They felt a sense of independence as now they did not need a parent or a guardian to drop or pick them up. A small change like this becomes a catalyst for greater things to come.

Leila Murgein, a 53-year-old student of the art-studio, born to a German mother and Yemini father was a case in point.

"What if she gets lost? There was no way I was going to let that happen," Leila's mother freaks out on me.

Her mother was in her 80s, and Leila was dependent on her for every little need.

"You will not be here forever. After you, what will happen?"

It took a while, but I convinced her mother to let her daughter take the metro on her own. Mrs. Murgein passed away in a couple of years.

Leila now travels to Germany on her own. She uses the metro regularly, and she meets friends at the mall for coffee.

I had to crack the whip often. My students realised that throwing a tantrum came with its consequences. I would emphasise that bad behaviour was not the norm and was unacceptable. Their art would grow in value if it came with a good, positive attitude.

Volunteers would want to overlook rudeness or rough behaviour. They, too, had to be trained to change their thinking. The entire attempt was to normalise the atmosphere as much as possible.

"We are hoping to raise the standards. We want society to treat them as artists and not just individuals with disability."

Chapter 35

Primary Colours

The beauty of Dubai is that it is a melting pot of different cultures. Most nationalities from different parts of the globe reside here.

James Casaki was a good example. He was British-Iraqi and my association with him was from my previous stints with DCSN and SFS.

Mawaheb was now almost four years old, and I wanted more students to come and join us. We had no monetary benefit in increasing enrollment as it was a non-profit organisation. My experience here had been so powerful and empowering that I wanted more individuals to avail of this opportunity.

I have always known the beauty of art, but the power of art as a medium of transformation was only realised in Mawaheb.

James had no interest in art. He was convinced he was no good at art. He was travelling to Spain on vacation, and I thought I would introduce him to Miro's work. Miro is a world-famous Spanish artist.

"What do you think?"

I whipped out my iPad and took him through several of Miro's creations.

Miro's artwork was simple and had a child-like feel to it. His use of primary colours and simple use of lines and shapes makes his work very relatable.

James was encouraged to go to see his work in Spain.

James was a good storyteller and on his return, I called him to speak about it with the students.

He loved Miro's work and spoke about it excitedly. He was now open to letting art take a place in his life.

"How would you draw, James?"

James was staring at a blank white canvas in front of him.

I helped him to interpret his life journey through art. Once he opened up to the idea and grew in confidence, there was no stopping him.

A year later, he had fifteen canvases ready and was invited to do solo exhibitions at mainstream art galleries. People actually paid for his art.

I, too, grew as a teacher. I started with a blank canvas. With time, the canvas saw not only shapes and colours but also life itself pour out from these canvases.

As the artists started believing in themselves, the world began believing in them.

Chapter 36

"I am the King."

"There is a war within and there is a war outside."

Jean - Michel Basquiat would be my chosen artist for the month. I did in-depth research on his work before unleashing him onto our artists.

He was a fearless and creative artist who rose to fame in the 1980s in New York. He used to be a musician and a graffiti artist and gradually became famous for his paintings.

His work was characterised as neo-expressionist. The neo-expression movement began taking shape in the late 1970s. It symbolised a shift from objectivity and minimalism to a subjective interpretation where the artist boldly and unabashedly created work that was an expression of how they saw the world. Anger, sadness and rebellion were expressed freely but fearlessly.

Deep down inside most of our artists realised they were different. Basquiat's style was subjective – he painted his emotions; he painted his pain. He was not looking to be objective. This stood out for me. Our artists I knew would instantly connect to this. They themselves saw the world differently. There were many battles they were fighting both on the outside and in their own heads. They needed a strong person and a phenomenal artist as an example to inspire them.

After my research was done, I decided to present his paintings to the class. We watched several videos of his work, his style, and his use of colour. The theme of the exhibition - 'I am who I am.'

The idea was to get each one of our artists to create one Basquiat inspired painting for our upcoming exhibition.

The eternal question, "Who am I?" I was convinced most of my students had never asked themselves this question. This was their time to dive deep.

What unfolded was fascinating – A young girl with Down syndrome replies, "I am who I am."

I again pressed on the question "Who are You?" A very petite looking Anju with down syndrome proudly presents her work. "Anju is the King" she says proudly. Her painting was a depiction of herself standing on a victory stand with a brush in her hand. She had separately drawn a crown as well.

Tiny and quiet, Anju views herself as the King, not the queen, mind you. She feels all-powerful.

Who am I? I began to bring a whole host of emotions and experiences to the fore. A young Iraqi man said, "There is a war within, and there is a war outside." The depth of his quote took me by surprise. His first painting depicted the war within. The war with his father, who could not accept his disability and emotionally abused him. The other painting was one of children and coffins - the war outside. It was about a recent terrorist attack on an army public school where hundreds of children were massacred.

Victor Sitali had a slightly hard time going within himself. He was our only artist who was not exactly special needs. He was audibly challenged.

"Who is Victor?" I gestured in sign language.

He stared back at me blankly. I repeated my question, asking him what he saw.

"I am an African guy, famous, patient, hard-working, who draws," He responded in sign language.

I forgot all about this and waited for him to finish his painting.

Victor is a deaf artist. His painting was an unusually big ear. It was a dramatic painting. It said it all. It spoke about his condition and how he felt about not being heard by the whole world. Few people know sign language, so it was hard for Victor to understand what he wanted to express.

Victor's expression was also about him wanting the world to see him just as an artist and not one who is audibly challenged.

Jean - Michel Basquiat has been a real inspiration to the class and me. We had several breakthroughs that day. It had been over thirty years to his death but his soul lives on, helping people find themselves.

"I am who I am" paintings were ready for an exhibition. The exhibition did well, and a lot of the paintings were sold.

Chapter 37

"Leila, Can You Draw a Hug"?

After some deliberation, I chose the Japanese artist, Yayoi Kusama, as my topic for research. Yayoi's life experiences, and the way she perceived life, was something our artists at the studio would connect with – Kusama led her life believing that nobody understood her. She came from a dysfunctional family. Her struggle with her mother who was not supportive of her creativity aggravated her mental illness.

Individuals with special needs face similar struggles. It would be unfair to say that most do not have supportive family structures, but the void and the isolation they feel are close to what Kusama experienced.

Kusama grew very fond of American artist, Georgia O'Keeffe's work and got in touch with her. Georgia was already well known for her paintings of enlarged flowers. She sent Georgia a few of her paintings. Georgia eventually wrote back encouraging her in every way possible. This is exactly the assurance and endorsement Kusama needed. This prompted her to move to New York in 1958.

The extensive use of polka dots in Kusama's installations is her trademark. As a child, she started gravitating towards painting after she experienced hallucinations, which often involved fields of dots. When she moved to New York, her early work came to be known as "Infinity Net" and constituted thousands of tiny dot-like marks which repeated themselves over and over, spreading across an undefined space, symbolic of a never-ending infinity.

She returned to Japan in 1973 but found herself in the throes of a crippling depression. She checked herself into a mental health facility and continued to live there, creating art all over again. Her art studio is within walking distance from the hospital in Tokyo, where she now resides.

'I am who I am' was answered by the students using Basquiat's work as their inspiration.

Leila, a 53-year-old artist at our studio, loved hugging people.

"Leila, can you draw a hug"? I asked.

I thought if I could somehow combine what came most naturally to a person, with a visual reference, and then asked the question "How do you connect to the world?" we might just end up with something very special.

Leila drew her version of a lady that appeared to resemble Kusama hugging multiple people. She drew multiple heart-shapes imprinted all over the long hugging arms. "Only love in the hugs" she exclaimed lovingly. Leila used the same vibrant colours that Kusama used in her work. The inspiration seemed to have rubbed off on her.

"What do you connect to?" I decided to probe a little further with the others.

It turned out that one of our female artists was grieving for her mother, and she had not even realised it.

She began painting, and what surfaced was a sense of anger. The pain was masked by the anger. She had been angry with her father for taking them to Egypt on a holiday, the timing of which coincided with her mother's death. She needed to blame someone for her pain and built this narrative that her father knew how ill her mother was and yet left her alone.

Miraculously, after completing her painting, she moved from anger to acceptance. Her father called me absolutely delighted. His daughter had hugged him for the first time in years.

Ironically, Kusama's brokenness as a person and contrastingly the brilliance of her art, had brought a father and daughter closer. Her dots were not in vain, someone else, somewhere else drew a line between those dots that helped them understand their own pain.

Another one of our artists, Anjana, was born a twin. She was on the autism spectrum, but her twin sister was not special needs, normal by societal standards.

Anjana would keep mouthing the words "I am a twin," but she in actual fact had no idea what being a twin meant.

I took her through all the stages of pregnancy, how a fetus actually begins forming, all the way to a full-grown pregnancy and the birth of a child. Children in her case. It truly sank in when she saw a visual representation of what twins in a womb look like.

She was now ready to get her creative juices flowing and get down to giving her Kusama inspired work the expression it deserved. She drew the entire nine month pregnancy cycle at various stages with a common umbilical cord connecting them. Now she finally belonged. She experienced her individuality at one level and felt the comfort of her twin identity at the same time.

We also had the case of a young man, an artist who had been addicted to pornography. On many occasions, he said, "I don't want to watch, but something makes me do it again and again."

"What do you like best about it?" I casually asked.

"Breasts," he said with certainty.

"Aha! So, you connect with breasts?"

He paused, naturally looking a little confused. He had never introspected, never given this any kind of thought. It was compulsive and addictive.

"Yes. When I look at pornography, I look only at the breasts. I only connect with the breasts."

He made it amply clear that no other body part worked for him quite like a woman's breasts.

I instinctively felt that our art therapy would help him.

He would painstakingly draw and re-draw, over and over again, a thousand breasts. His painting was called "The land of a thousand boobs."

At the end of a month from the day we spoke, he was totally over his pornography addiction. A thousand boobs later, he had grown tired and had normalised it. He was over it, and it seemed pointless to him.

The Yayoi Kusama-inspired theme 'Connections' actually helped this young man connect with himself and break him away from the shackles of a distorted and obsessive idea of sexuality. This was truly ironic as Kusama herself had a huge struggle coming to terms with male sexuality. We suspect the root cause of her fear of intimacy was the loveless marriage between her parents and her having experienced her father's womanising. She could never quite make her connection with this aspect of her life.

Top: *The Mawaheb team with all our amazing volunteers* | Center: *Celebrating happy times*
Bottom: *Our Mawaheb artists dressed as Frida Khalo*

A Fun day painting the walls and ourselves

CSR events with various corporates

Fun days at Mawaheb, while I was teaching them life skills through art, my students were teaching me about life

Various events at Mawaheb - talking, eating, dancing, workshopping and always having a blast

Chapter 38

In Black and White

The pandemic came like a wave of uncertainty, a disrupter of the highest order. People across the planet woke up to realise the frailty of life. All the so called well laid plans went out of the window. For the first time we realised that plans meant living in the future and the future never looked bleaker.

Zeheer and I were among those who felt its impact. Whoever imagined that an emergency visit to India at the beginning of March 2020 meant that we would not be able to get back to Dubai for a full four months? Worse still, since this was supposed to be a short trip, we decided to leave Zara behind with the very capable and trustworthy Saraswati, our house help and support system.

After my return to Dubai in the middle of 2020, Mawaheb decided to shut shop. We had no idea if we would reopen in better times.

They say in every adversity lies an opportunity. Two of our talented artists, Abdulla Lutfi, aged 31 and Asma Baker, aged 35, decided that I should personally mentor them. I was honoured and excited to be a part of their journey, helping them grow as people and being the catalyst in furthering their careers as artists with special needs.

Asma and Abdulla were both local Emirati talent and had gained a fair bit of popularity as artists.

Abdulla looked at the world in black and white and a lot of his artwork is a representation of this view, using only black and white as the vehicle for his expression. His forte, his attention to detail.

He is on the autism spectrum and his art is a representation of how he views the world as a person of special needs. At the age of 30, Abdulla has already achieved a lot by way of sold-out solo exhibitions, commissioned work from hotels and various corporate houses. Additionally, he has collaborated with a variety of other artists.

His sharp sense of humour added to the overall persona. Abdulla had gradually begun to understand that his success was not only his but belonged to the collective community of individuals with special needs. People like Abdulla have played a huge part in changing the perception of how 'normal' people view people with disability.

When I began to privately mentor him in December 2020, he was already a very big name. As his fame grew, so did the demand for his work. Individuals and organisations had begun vying for his work and began getting in touch with us. Abdulla was now being taken far more seriously simply for his art and not just as an artist with special needs.

This, however, came with its own set of challenges. Clients required him to attend and actively participate in meetings. After all, he was going to create the magic they had envisioned.

Abdulla would at times fall asleep, burp and exhibit what would be deemed as 'unprofessional' behaviour in the normal professional world. This is where I had to step in and make him aware of the importance of a client asking for his time and taking the time out of their busy schedule to meet him.

"Why do I have to come to meetings? Art is my job."

It took time but with persistence, Abdulla did turn the corner. He finally realised that he no longer could afford to be another misunderstood person with disability. These were clients, some of them high paying clients - they had a right to have expectations. Abdulla and I worked towards making this happen. I played my role as creative guide and a behavioural specialist.

Asma Baker is now a motivational speaker. However, there was a time when she refused to speak and had trouble verbalising. She struggled to understand herself as a person and her identity as an individual on the autism spectrum. She simply refused to talk.

"I have one condition if I am going to work with you" I laid it down in no uncertain terms.

Asma looked at me. I let the thought linger.

"You have to talk. I need you to connect with me. I need you to talk to me."

I was aware that she was probably going through depression, and not wanting to talk was her way of withdrawing from the world. It had become second nature, and somehow, I would have to help her pull herself out of this.

"How can I help you if I don't know what you are thinking?"

Asma really wanted to work with me, and I hoped the gentle pressure I was deliberately exerting on her would work.

Asma slowly began opening up to me. She explained that 'thinking from the heart' really helped her understand the world better. It helped her perceive what others were going through as well. The experience of thinking from the heart, as she calls it, led her to poetry writing. She went ahead and published a book of poems titled "Heart and mind."

She was someone who had chosen to isolate herself and was constantly afraid of being judged. Asma worked hard on transforming herself and went on to become a motivational speaker, an artist, an entrepreneur and a poet.

In her own words - "I love to inspire people, speaking of my life journey as a person who has special needs. For me, to be a motivational speaker is to inspire the students in schools and colleges, to tell them about how our community is slowly changing and accepting people of determination as part of this world. I want to show them that people of determination are amazing and fun people to know, and the world can learn so much from them."

Asma got an opportunity to work with Special Olympics 2019 to interact with experts in the field and several individuals with special needs. She recited her poems in front of huge audiences, and a song she wrote was played on the opening night of the Special Olympics.

Asma became a known name after her appearance at the Special Olympics and has been invited by several educational institutions of repute to narrate her inspirational story.

I am proud to mentor her. I often feel she has contributed manifold to my life, perhaps, in more ways than I could ever imagine.

Asma and Abdulla, by achieving all they have, have become the poster children for the special needs community. When people like me champion this cause, I do see it making a difference, but this community badly needs more Asmas and Abdullas spreading their own message and demonstrating the "normal", that the neurotypical folk need. The special needs community may walk differently but they can walk shoulder to shoulder with the normal folk. We truly have a lot to learn from them.

Top Left: *Asma signing her book* | Top Right: *Our first day at the new studio, The Next Chapter*
Bottom Left: *Asma's Book* | Bottom Left: *Abdulla, Asma, Victor and Zahra on our trip to Washington DC*

The mentee with his mentor

Chapter 39

The Journey

On the 9th of March 2020, we received news that my mother-in-law had passed away in Mumbai. The first wave of the coronavirus had just begun gaining momentum. We were to return to Dubai after the funeral and the ten-day prayers that followed.

It was all planned, but we found ourselves in a situation - a lot of countries, including the UAE, had closed their borders. We tried every route that was available, but we just could not find a way back.

Luckily we had our home in Mumbai and my husband's office understood our predicament and were very supportive. The real cause for alarm was that we had left Zara behind with our trusted caretaker Saraswati. Other than that trip to London we had never left Zara alone with anyone.

Fifteen days passed, and we were told it was another fifteen days before we could get back.

Fifty days had now passed. The situation in India was going from bad to worse. There was a massive surge in the number of infected cases all over the world. This was going to be the long haul.

This nightmarish period had another damning effect on me. It transported me back in time to when Zara, as an infant, had been confirmed as an individual with special needs.

I recall this incident when we were visiting Mumbai and casually walking around our beautiful colony.

"How is your daughter?" A couple known to us decides to inquire

"Jenai's fine. She is in school. Busy with her studies," I knew they wanted to know more about Zara, but I spoke about Jenai.

"No, the younger one. The retarded one" The word retarded came out nonchalantly.

"You don't need to say that. All you had to do was ask how Zara is."

"Actually, we have no idea how to address her."

The couple looked rather sheepish and replied feebly.

My anger subsided and gave way to a solid realisation. People have no idea how to approach this. There is negligible information on special needs. Something had to be done.

I made a few flyers and circulated them around the area. I was going to have a talk on special needs. To be honest, I estimated at best twenty-five odd residents to show up for this.

To my surprise, more than a hundred people were in attendance.

This became a turning point of sorts as it paved the way for the formation of another support group, the Ahura support group.

It began as a group providing vocational training, and with time, it became a full-fledged support with parental involvement and volunteers. Regular meetings, parties, and other gatherings meant that at least a few individuals within the special needs community were able to be assisted, find a sense of belonging, and lead better lives.

The unpleasant interaction with the couple was perhaps needed to mobilise this.

The present always has an uncanny ability to pull you back. The truth was that we were in Mumbai in the year 2020, in the middle of a crisis and feeling rather stuck.

Our first concern was Zara being there without either Zeheer or me. Our bigger concern was whether Zara or Saraswati would get infected with COVID. This would prove catastrophic as Zara had specific timings for medication, and only Saraswati, in our absence, could handle this. The very thought terrified us.

"Are you even trying hard enough to leave?"

As well-meaning as my friends from Mumbai were, they somehow made me feel like I wasn't doing enough to try and get back to my daughter, and that really hurt.

"What are you saying? Just a few days ago, a friend and his wife successfully got back to Dubai."

"I would never have been able to stay away from my child this long."

Zeheer and I were extremely anxious and were really having a hard time trying to come to terms with this. These stray comments aggravated our stress levels.

Thankfully, the absolute opposite was happening in Dubai. Our friends, Tanaz and Rehan, who are like family, stood by us like rocks. They visited Zara every single day in our absence. It was the lockdown period, and only three people could be in a car at any given time. This did not stop them from taking Saraswati and Zara for a drive every day within the confines of the Arabian Ranches, the complex where we lived. They would also help with groceries and other essentials. This was a real blessing in those horrid times.

It was a full one hundred and twenty days before we could actually return to Dubai. We would finally be reunited with our younger daughter.

I always had this belief that we were indispensable to Zara and that she would simply not be able to live without us, but spending this time away from her totally shattered that myth.

The truth is, the world will go on, and I can hardly believe these words as I say them. Zara will find her way. I am convinced she will be fully taken care of if and when we are not here to care for her.

The 'Oh God, please take her before us' line of thinking has slowly vanished. The many days spent apart had shown me that nature has its way of taking care of the most troublesome situations. Not one of us is indispensable.

Left: *Saraswati with Zara* | **Right:** *Tanaz, Rehan, Zeheer, Zara and I*

Chapter 40

Dolphins

My mother-in-law had lived a full life. Her funeral was a testimony to the same. People were waiting to meet us and offer their condolences. My older daughter Jenai insisted that she had something to tell us and that it simply could not wait. I tried to reason with her; a number of people, all well-wishers, needed to be attended to; surely this could wait.

"This is important."

Jenai pulled out a sonography report and looked at us excitedly. On the day of my mother-in-law's funeral, my daughter informed us that she was pregnant with her first baby! Life certainly moves in mysterious ways. If one could feel sad and happy at the same time, this was the moment. My husband and I had barely set foot back in India, still processing the loss of his mother, and my daughter, on that very day, told us we were to become grandparents. What are the odds?

Dating back a couple of months prior to this bitter-sweet moment we were experiencing, Jenai's workplace decided to take the employees for an outing, an office picnic. They would get on a ferry boat from the gateway of India and sail into the Arabian Sea just off the coast of Mumbai.

As they were sailing, a pod of dolphins began following their boat for some length of time, an extremely rare occurrence in this part of the world. At first my daughter thought this to just be a coincidence but it became more than apparent that they were being continuously followed by this pod of dolphins.

She became curious and began learning more about dolphin behaviour. Dolphins apparently have the ability to connect with the unborn fetus, and this is the reason why they follow the boat. Interestingly, Jenai had no idea that she was pregnant and sure enough, on a medical investigation, she was told she was a few months into pregnancy.

When I heard of this, my memory quickly sprinted back to the month of May in the year 1989. My husband was in the merchant navy and we were sailing across the Bosphorus in Turkey. The captain called a few of us on the bridge and just then, a pod of dolphins began following our ship. At first, we were just soaking in this once in a lifetime moment.

"Gulshan, you are pregnant."

The captain said this to me, looking me right in the eye unhesitatingly. He did not say, "You may be pregnant" or "Chances are, you are pregnant." The suddenness of his comment and the certainty in his tone threw me off. I, in fact, was pregnant with Jenai. I think I did a good job of acting surprised, as I had not informed anyone on board just yet.

I learnt something marvel worthy, all thanks to my pregnancy. The well informed captain went onto explain that dolphins are blessed with the power of echolocation, which gives them ability to sense if a woman is pregnant, but only if she is present in the water or sailing in the water. Apparently, they can actually see the baby in the womb. This ability is what drew them to me. They, it seems wanted to communicate with the unborn baby.

Top Left: *Rehan's first scan* | Top Right: *As soon as Jenai told us about her pregnancyr*
Bottom Left: *Jenai sailing* | Bottom Left: *The dolphin sighting*

Chapter 41

The Celebrity and the Celebrated

The one hundred and twenty days we spent in my husband's family home in Mumbai turned out to be more positive than we had imagined. We were witness to our daughter's growing belly, her beautiful glowing face, and most of all, experiencing those magical moments of her pregnancy. It almost made up for all the time we never really had with her because of our preoccupation with Zara.

During the same time, at a three hour flying distance from Mumbai, in my adopted home, Dubai, the support group I had started a few years ago, Special Families Support Group (SFS) began feeling my absence. The students at the Mawaheb art studio were also feeling rather uncertain about what life would have to offer after the pandemic.

It had taken a lot of blood, sweat and tears to build both of these organisations. In some form, both SFS and Mawaheb had become the lifeline for not only individuals with special needs but for their families and caretakers too.

Working cultures all over the world were rapidly making the switch to online platforms. Work from home was here to stay.

It was important for me to find a way to keep SFS going. This was certainly a cause of worry but I also knew things would fall into place, somehow.

I reasoned with myself, "I have a home. Apart from not being able to travel and other COVID-related restrictions, we were comfortable."

The largest film industry in the world, Bollywood, was right there in my backyard, so to speak. It occurred to me that there could be no better way to mobilise the support group than have its members connect with their on-screen idols via video conferencing. My resourceful sister Roxane managed to connect us to a whole host of talented actors in the industry.

It was my idea and yet I was nervous. I had to talk to them, brief them about the concept, keeping in mind that they had never interacted with hundreds of individuals with special needs at one go, in a single programme. They were quite apprehensive at first but eventually all of them agreed to give it a go.

"They will share their life journey with you. It will mean a lot to them. They just want you to listen. Your presence matters."

This was all I said to our celebrity guests. We began the journey with Arshad Warsi, a well-known actor in the Indian film industry, and it worked out very well. The kids and their families loved the interaction. They logged on in large numbers and poured their hearts out.

In the days to follow, we had many more sessions. Before I knew it, we had done over a dozen Zoom sessions with well-known actors and actresses.

It turned out to be a transformational experience for the celebrities as well. A lot of them had tears in their eyes. They admitted to feeling bad about having so many apprehensions when I had asked them to do this. They were habituated to donning their entertainer identities. All they had to do was just be there for someone, nothing more was expected of them. This experience of just being themselves despite the celebrity status blew their mind away.

It was beautiful to see the invisible walls of doubt, fear, and awe completely breaking down between the most celebrated people in the 'normal' world and the special individuals in the world of special needs. The celebrities humbly sat there patiently listening to every individual, answering them and watching them take on centre stage, boldly exhibiting their dance moves. They helped them feel like superstars in their own right. Our participants felt heard, endorsed and cared for. Furthermore, this gave them the confidence to proudly flaunt their identity as individuals belonging to the special needs community.

I was taken aback by the overwhelming success of these Zoom interactions. If it had not been for the devastating effects of the pandemic, the lockdown by itself would have been a blessing, as all of this would never have happened. In fact, buoyed by the amazing outcome of the SFS interactions, I confidently went ahead and set up similar Zoom interactions for our artists at Mawaheb.

For our artists, I thought it best to get in touch with artists of repute from countries like France, Poland, and Spain. They, too, were happy to interact and inspire our talented lot at the studio.

Chapter 42

True Friendship and a Flying Kiss

A short while ago, I had just finished speaking with Rehan, our little grandson who lives in Mumbai, over our regular video calls. It amazed me to witness that after every video call, he would only give Zara a flying kiss. Amusingly, despite our many pleas, he refused to send even a single kiss our way.

I recall the time we would take Zara to the mall when babies under two years of age would turn their heads and look at her. They would look right into her eyes like there was some connection.

There is something about Zara and the little children.

Whenever this happens, my heart smiles, immediately connecting it with Jas, our neighbour's daughter and the truest friend Zara has ever had or will have.

Jas is seven months younger than Zara.

"Can I take Zara for a movie?" A young high school-going Jas asks us.

Zeheer and I were totally caught off guard and, to be honest, rather stumped at this request. We were simply not used to this.

Zeheer was rather uncomfortable, but at the same time, one could not ignore the genuineness of her desire.

A middle ground was found which would satisfy all parties involved. Zeheer suggested that Jas and Zara sit in the back rows further away from the screen and we would seat ourselves in the front rows. He did not want us to come in the way of the friends' day out experience.

The movie in question was Gravity and to slightly complicate matters it was 3D. The seating arrangements agreed upon, the movie commences but Zeheer it seemed preferred to watch a different movie called Zara. He kept turning his head to the back rows to check on Zara. Gravity, 3D was completely lost on him.

Zara did not fancy the 3D glasses. All we could notice was Zara flinging the glasses, not wanting to put them on, and Jas devotedly picked them up from the floor and placed them back on Zara. This went on for quite a while.

"Jas, did you enjoy the film?"

"I enjoyed it," she smiled back.

I can say with certainty, forget enjoying; poor Jas must not have gotten to watch three back-to-back scenes without a disturbance.

Jas never hesitated to take Zara for dinner with her friends. It was not a matter of concern to Jas that her friends had never encountered or spent time with an individual with special needs. She would order Nasi Goreng, Zara's favourite dish and feed her. Jas's way of normalising and integrating Zara into her life was so comforting.

"When I graduate, I will take Zara with me, make her walk alongside me as I collect my certificate."

Unfortunately, this dream did not come true as Jas graduated in 2020 and this just could not be made possible.

I hope Zara can instead be her best lady on Jas's special day.

The 3 friends Jas, Zara and Poojitha all born in the same year 1997

Chapter 43

"I Feel Left Out"

Zara is now practically as tall as me and weighs nearly forty kilograms. Try as I might, lifting her was out of the question.

My husband and Saraswati took over, and for that, I cannot thank them enough. However, it led me to the scary thought, "Would she still have a connection with me?"

"Let me try and shift her," I said to Zeheer. I could not give up. The fear of 'losing' her drove me to try harder.

I had to finally accept this was not happening, heartbreakingly so.

She does respond and reach out to Zeheer and Saraswati. He still carries her on his back. She gets three seizures a month at times, yet between my husband and Saraswati, they leave no stone unturned. I am blessed, but despite that, and I hate to say this, I feel left out.

Chapter 44

"Thank God, ME!."

<hr>

It has been quite a journey, a journey I never signed up for in the first place.

As I lie awake on my bed in the stillness of this vast Arabian desert, a thought creeps in through the silence: was my life meant to be 'normal'? Part of a happy family unit with the predictable highs, lows and the mostly in-between's?

And then, one day, a seemingly harmless seizure took it all away.

Back then, it felt like the almighty had punished me, kicked me in the gut and stolen the life I was supposed to have. I allow myself that generous dollop of self-pity, and then, somehow, I smile.

This is my destiny. It was meant to be. There is no other way it could have been. And now, I say there is no other way it should be.

Tossing and turning on my bed, there are miles to go before I sleep, miles to go before I sleep.

In the past, I would often wonder about the thousands of miles this body, heart and mind have travelled in this journey with Zara. Despite all that I have mentioned about indispensability, I still get the odd pang of anxiety just thinking about what would happen to Zara if she outlived us. Then I say to myself, "Que sera sera, what will be, will be!"

From the screaming, the anger, and the hurt, "Why Me?" to perhaps this is my destiny and a feeble acknowledgement "Why Not Me?"

It's been twenty-seven years to Zara's birth. The 5th of May 1997, the day Zara was born, seems a lifetime away. It has taken me a very long time to understand that this is what I am chosen for. Truth be told, on some days it still continues to be a long hard struggle but today I am a different person and I can say with certainty that acceptance and gratitude have found their way into my life, "Thank God, ME!."

"If you can't find one, start one"

These words changed my life.
They can change yours too!

'Be kind': Podcast launched in UAE gives voice to people with disabilities

New podcast shares how people with special needs in the UAE handle bullying and overcome adversity with community support

Ramola Talwar Badam
Dubai
15 July, 2024

 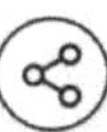

A podcast has been launched by a Dubai special needs advocate to empower people with disabilities so they can speak directly about their challenges.

PODcastbygulshan

Welcome to the PODcast by Gulshan, where POD stands for People of Determination.

Join host Gulshan Kavarana as she interviews remarkable individuals who have overcome adversity and achieved success against all odds. Each episode features inspiring stories, insightful conversations, and valuable lessons from PODs who embody resilience, strength, and determination. Tune in to discover the triumphs, challenges, and journeys of these extraordinary individuals on their path to success.

Follow us on Instagram

For updates and behind-the-scenes content:

POD.castbyGulshan

Channel Details

www.youtube.com/@podcastbygulshanKavarana

Write to Me

gulshankavarana@gmail.com